The Nature of
Story and Creativity

By Hugh Steven

Printed in the United States of America.

Unless otherwise noted, Scripture quotations are taken from The Holy Bible, New Interna-
tional version © 1973,1978 1984 International Bible Society. Used by permission of Zondervan
Publishing House. All rights reserved. Scripture quotations marked KJV are from the King
James Version.

ISBN: 0-9769634-0-X

Library of Congress Cataloging-in-Publication is pending

Steven, Hugh. The Nature of Story and Creativity 2005 by Hugh Steven ISBN: 0-9769634-0-X
Self-help, Creative writing, Biography, Autobiography, Memoirs.

Cover design by Jewel Fink

Interior design by Stephen Board

Dedication

To All Those Who Are Touched and Fascinated
by the Miracle of Language and the Written Word.

Introduction and Appreciation

Early in my writing career, Earl Adams, a longtime Wycliffe colleague, suggested I write a syllabus on writing. The purpose, he said, would be to "help and encourage our Wycliffe colleagues to tell their stories." So began the adventure of synthesizing my ideas, experiences and observations about the nature of language and the creative process. I wanted to explore the so-called mystery of imaginative creativity that can emerge out of a writer's thoughtful reflection and research.

As I matured as a writer, I was able to test my theories and material (often in developing stages) through a series of writers' workshops. These included being a guest lecturer at a number of colleges and universities that included, Regent College, Biola University, and Trinity Western University, as well as in several cross-cultural venues.

My wife Norma is, in her own right, a writer, published author and editor. Together we conducted writers' workshops in Australia, Canada, Singapore, Mexico, and for the Inuit Eskimo people in Kotzebue, Alaska sponsored by the Kotzebue Museum of Anthropology. Besides presenting this material in weeklong workshops and seminars, I participated in many one-day workshops with other writers and editors. I have also acted as a formal and informal mentor and facilitator to encourage several Wycliffe colleagues and others who needed guidance and help in publishing their own books and articles.

At this point, I need to stress that I do not have a handy-dandy ten-point chart that says, "Follow these rules and you will become a world-class writer." What I do present in this book are suggestions and principles that have worked for me as a published author of over thirty books and more than two hundred articles and profile pieces.

While I believe writing is an art form that comes from deep within a person's essence, I also believe it is a craft that can be sharpened and improved with the applications of certain techniques. For example, for a writer to remain fresh within his or her art he or she has a responsibility to be a curious explorer, an avid reader, a keen observer of the human comedy, with a willingness to share ideas and interpretations. By definition this means there is always more to learn about the weightier matters that include justice, mercy and faith. However, in each case, the writer must explore how these abstract concepts are made concrete in deeds, attitudes and acts of love. C.S. Lewis argued that it was picture language and stories that came the closest to grasping the concreteness of reality, including God's overwhelming reality.

I need to confess that with every new writing project, I am keenly aware of G.R. Elton's words from his book, The Practice of History:

The more the historians know, the more [he or she] despairs of his ability to tell it, for the sheer complexity of the historical process stands inexorably in the way.

Most every writer I know, myself included, identifies with these words and occasionally experiences writer's block. At such times Elton's words can lodge themselves in the mind as a mocking reminder of one's self-doubt and vulnerability. But then, a friend, a spouse or colleague comes along and emboldens you with affirming words about your work, plus a reminder that with God's help all things are possible.

For such words of encouragement I here once again thank Stephen Board, a true friend and colleague who, without remuneration acted as editor, typesetter and encourager. To Jim Wylie who loves nothing better than to find typos and spelling errors I thank him for his careful scrutiny of the book. To Jewel Fink, Wycliffe colleague, who, for the second time designed a cover for one of my books. I am most grateful to her for her creative artistic skill and spiritual energy. To Norma's niece, Sheryl St. Gelais, an educator, I offer a special word of appreciation for

her careful critiquing of the bound galleys and for her positive reinforcement that the book should be published.

And I here thank my wife Norma who has been a faithful and patient
partner in the editing and critiquing of most of my previous books.
However, since her stroke she has been unable to make me look better
than I am. Nonetheless, I again thank her for her all the years she acted
as an insightful editor, my best friend and full partner in our writing
ministry with Wycliffe Bible Translators.

Finally, since no story is told in isolation and certainly our ministry
with Wycliffe did not happen in isolation, I here offer a special word of
gratitude to those who, after our "retirement" from Wycliffe, continued
to be our prayer and financial partners. Your faithfulness allowed me to
bring this volume and the last volume of the William Cameron
Townsend biography to completion. In every way you are co-authors
with God in the writing of our books and of every story that might be
written as a result of this book. We could not have done it without you.
My special thanks also, to Billy Gibson his wife Patty and son James for
their encouragement and practical financial help in the publishing of
this book.

Hugh Steven

Table of Contents

Prologue

I was once told a story about a young woman who had an early school experience that might easily have happened to some of you. One day a young married woman invited a former classmate, whom she hadn't seen for several years, to her home for lunch. As she took her friend's coat and invited her into the living room, the friend noticed several paintings hanging on the walls. "These are beautiful!" said the woman. "Who painted them?" Her hostess smiled. "I did," "How wonderful, I never knew you could paint. When did you begin?" "That's an interesting story."

"When I was in the seventh grade, I was doodling on a piece of paper and didn't hear the teacher's instructions. When the teacher noticed I wasn't paying attention, she became angry and marched down the aisle to my seat, grabbed my paper and held it up to the class and said, 'Look, class, this is a picture of someone who is going absolutely nowhere,' and flung the drawing back on my desk.

"That experience so inhibited me, so devastated my self-esteem, that I determined never to draw another picture. It wasn't until I was married and began to feel good about my role as wife and mother that my husband noticed my interest in art and painting and encouraged me to pursue my artistic interests. With his help I did. These paintings are the result."

I am not sure if this is a factual story, since I heard it from another person. But like myths and fairy tales, this story contains a deep truth about the nature of creativity and how children learn. First, it supports the long-held notion that children cannot perform well until they begin to feel good about themselves. But in order for a child to feel good about himself/herself, educators have learned that a child needs to have one parent or an adult who stands beside them to offer encouragement in their projects. Positive reinforcement indeed works.

I can personally attest to this. As a young teenager I was ridiculed and became the butt of jokes because I once commented to some of my friends that I thought the gentle waves on our beach looked like leaves turning over in a book. It wasn't until I told my feelings of rejection and shame to a wise old gentleman with wire-rimmed glasses, bib overalls and plastered-down hair, that I felt affirmed. He said I shouldn't be ashamed for thinking differently than my friends because he, too, thought waves looked like leaves turning over in a book. He was our school janitor!

However, some educators argue that children will not feel good about themselves until they first begin to perform well. In an effort to boost self-esteem, a child may be told they are wonderful no matter what they do. This may lead them to the logical conclusion that it really doesn't matter what they do. This, of course, sends a wrong-headed message to young people.

Leonard Woodcock supports the second lesson I gained from this story in an essay entitled, *The Natural History of the American Writer.* Woodcock said that American writers have three common characteristics in their background:

> The first is that they have had an experience of loss, or isolation from other children in childhood. That experience might have been something like an illness that kept them isolated from other children for a period. It could have been the loss of a parent, or a dear friend or even a pet, and indeed the loss of self-esteem. The second characteristic is that they read a lot. The third

is that they had someone who overtly encouraged them to develop their writing skills.

I believe the average person is more talented, more intelligent and more creative than they probably feel they are. I am also convinced that because of peer pressure, and the fear of being marked down, criticized or made to feel foolish, many people are fearful of sharing their literary gifts. One of the great blocks to creativity is the fear of being embarrassed. The young girl who was told by the teacher she would never amount to anything was marked down, rejected, intimidated and embarrassed and that became a serious block to her creativity. It took an empathetic person whom she trusted to encourage and support her in her art.

There have been some interesting studies done on embarrassment and the way children learn. It seems that students during the first through third grades in school ask ninety percent of the questions. By the fourth grade, this number is reversed. It is the teacher who now asks most of the questions.

The principal reason for this shift is that between the first and third grades, children have learned to conform to a group. They are now afraid to be as individualistic as they once were. Their natural inquisitiveness and playfulness have given way to rules, conformity and judicial thinking over intuition. Notice how many teenagers have to wear clothing that is "cool" and accepted by their peer group. This often results in the student's innate creativity being lost, covered up and inhibited.

I was interested to learn that Elvis Presley played an enormous part in releasing the inhibitions of many young people in the fifties by wearing extravagant clothing like purple shirts and loud pants to high school. Presley did this in the face of his peers who told him it wasn't cool to wear the same kind of clothing as black people. But Presley was his own man. He knew if he wanted to realize his dream and satisfy his deep itch to perform he could not cover up his creativity by conforming to the herd.

It is my hope that this book will in some way help you to uncover and release your covered-up creativity. I encourage you to jettison whatever it is that is making you feel self-conscious about your gifts.

While I sincerely want to be an encouragement and help to you, in the final analysis, no matter how much others or I would like to help you, you must walk that "yellow brick road" by yourself. The only way you will learn to write is to write. I also hope you will come to understand that writing is a craft that takes concentration and hard, solitary work even for the person who enjoys working with words and concepts.

If there is a magic formula in becoming a writer, it is that you will learn your craft by wanting to learn, by having a passion and desire to write, and then doing it. Persistence and desire always win over raw, undisciplined talent. If you feel you have a desire to write but don't know where to begin, I offer the chapters on the creative attitude as a possible first step in the development of your life as a writer.

Hugh Steven
Santa Ana, California

Chapter One

The Nature of Story

Human Beings *are story-telling animals and God is a story-telling God. To outgrow the story, is to outgrow our humanity.*

A. The Nature of Story

Dr. Robert Longacre, a longtime friend, colleague, poet and linguist extraordinaire, who has written and taught extensively on the principles of discourse analysis, gave me the following definition of the true nature of story:

> A story is not an essay or sermon, or a food recipe or a set of procedures. A story has a story line, that is, a succession of happenings that are recounted. Of necessity, story has participants involved in some sort of struggle, however refined or crude; story has to bring such a struggle to a head, to resolve it in some way, even if the resolution is not a happy one.

I was pleased Longacre said that story is not a sermon. In a traditional sermon, a preacher usually expounds a particular biblical passage point by point. He or she then draws specific conclusions about the meaning or moral of the passage. Most often the passage is explained in overt Christian language that reveals biblical virtue and harmony. The sermon can, and often is (like story) supported with anecdotes drawn from history, literature, current events or personal experiences. But seldom does a sermon leave room for ambiguity or mystery. Usually in a sermon a preacher or essayist tells us what he or she thinks.

The distinctive feature about the nature of story is that the characters (participants) reveal the meaning of the narrative by their actions, words they speak and choices they make. In a way, the storyteller stands to one side and allows the reader to discover or interpret the story for him or herself. The storyteller shows us the meaning of the story through the use of description, specific details, metaphor, imagery, dialogue, symbolic language and story line or plot. There are times, of course, when a writer may speak in his or her own voice as one of the characters to make the moral of the story plain. But even in such cases, the character is "on stage," engaged in some form of dramatic dialogue.

B. In Story, Something Happens

Story is also concerned with a good unity of opposites, or a continuous interlocking theme throughout, with lots of cause and effect. This allows the reader to be caught up in the drama and excitement of the story and left at the conclusion with a sense of satisfaction. Longacre's term is a *succession of happenings.* By this, he means that every story has motion (action), that the character(s) are doing things, going somewhere and thinking thoughts. Story has a point; it can illustrate an idea, or emphasize the folly of a bad decision. All stories need a storyteller who selects details, anecdotes, and metaphors for a specific audience. My personal view of the nature of story is summed up in a quote I once read that said:

> Every good story that entertains without enriching is superficial and escapist. The story that enriches without entertaining is simply dull. The story that does both is a delight.

In order to make a story a delight, the storyteller must use dramatic storytelling techniques. Mark Masse, who teaches at the University of Oregon, echoes my feelings about the nature of creative storytelling when he says:

> A good creative nonfiction writer will transcend the conventions of fact-based journalism by portraying characters with psycho-

logical depth, providing riveting details and descriptions, and presenting a true -story [based upon verifiable facts] that uses dramatic scenes to engage the reader's interest and emotions.[1]

C. No Story Without Conflict

In a word, the basis of effective drama in story is conflict. The secret of all great love stories, for example, is an obstacle. That is, some kind of barrier or conflict must exist between the two lovers that both in some way have to overcome. I once wrote a biography about two young people who were carrying on a long-distance romance in two different countries. When I researched the story I had the good fortune to have both the young woman's private diary and letters written to the man with whom she was in love. After comparing the woman's diary entry dates with letters written to the man whom she one day hoped would propose marriage, it was clear she was more serious about making a commitment than was he. Inexplicably he often wrote letters telling her about a particular girl he had dated and even kissed good night. When I compared the letter she wrote in response to this bit of news it was fairly conciliatory and magnanimous. She even agreed with the premise that it might be a good idea for both of them to date other people. However, when I compared her diary entry concerning this revelation there was no such magnanimity. She poured out her soul to her diary as to an intimate friend about how anxious, angry and frustrated she was that he didn't understand how much she loved him and how deeply he had hurt her with his insensitivity.

This is a classic example of a person outwardly controlling her feelings before the world, but inwardly suffering intense emotional anguish. Such tension generates drama on two planes. One is the interplay between the controlled outer activities of the character as it clashes with the individual's inner anguish and turmoil. It is this clash of two opposing forces that makes for drama. And it has nothing to do with TV's amazing videos that show people jumping out of windows to escape a burning building, or big rigs racing on a dirt track and crashing into one another. When William Faulkner won the Nobel Prize he said

---

1 Mark H. Masse, Creative Nonfiction, *Where Journalism and Storytelling Meet* (Boston, *The Writer,* October, 1995), p. 15.

in his acceptance speech that the central human drama was *the human heart in conflict with itself.*

D.   No Story Without Emotion

Charles Dickens was once asked about the artistic principles by which he wrote. He said, "I have only one artistic principle, that is, to rouse the emotions of my readers." Still the question remains, how does a writer tap the emotions of a subject after the fact? One answer is to ask the right kind of question. If a friend has just returned from China or the coast of Spain, the Grand Canyon, or the Swiss Alps, ask how it felt to be in the Alps on a spring morning with a profusion of wild flowers in bloom. Ask what a person thought and felt about the birth of their own child after seeing their grandchild for the first time.

1. Dramatic Characterization

Emotion will automatically follow when you employ dramatic characterization. If you show a wealthy slum lord evicting a widow with six stair-step children in midwinter, you don't have to editorialize and tell the reader the slum lord is a merciless, malevolent, hardhearted scoundrel. The reader will interpret the slum lord's character through his actions.

It is through dramatic characterization that the reader comes to know a character's personality, worldview, attitudes, and relationships he or she has with family, colleagues and friends. It's helpful to remember that emotion is at the heart of all art. That is, it is the everyday emotions of panic, fear, frustration, tenderness, nervousness, jealousy, humor, kindness, being tired and overwhelmed and more, that identifies the hero of the story as being a human like ourselves.

E.   What is Plot?

The simplest definition of plot is that it is an account of characters and events, or a succession of happenings (action) that builds over time and moves through conflict toward resolution. Stories are always about particular people and experiences. Therefore, for a story to be a story, it must revolve around characters trying to resolve a problem, or going in search of something. This is often called a quest myth. In the quest, the main character goes on a journey and encounters problems that he or she must overcome or be overcome by them. The plot of the story develops through a series of problems, how they occur, and how they are resolved. The most dramatic moments for the hero in the story are the crisis points where the character comes into conflict with a problem and is forced to make a decision that will reveal the individual's strengths or weaknesses.

1. The Journey is the Story

The suspense and pleasure of story occurs on the journey with its surprises, unforeseen pitfalls, twists and turns, the love interests, suspense, danger and all the challenges for risk and choice that reveal the true essence of an individual. Without the journey there is no goal and thus, no story. The elements of story plot have always been the interaction between character and action, or between places and people.

2. Drama, Character, Action

A tongue-in-cheek example of what I mean by the interaction of drama, character and action occurs when your male character says to a woman, "I love you." That statement by itself has no intrinsic story line or drama. It's simply a pleasant sentiment that many people tell one another every day. However, a story begins (or the plot thickens) when you add action and conflict. Suppose, after telling the woman he loves her, the man says, "Let's elope." And the woman says, "Great, but what about your wife?" Now you have a problem with conflict that needs to be resolved. Just as fire is necessary to explode the heavy pine cones to release the seeds for the next batch of pine trees, so too, without conflict, or in some cases a "trial by fire" a person cannot reveal his inner character. Most often it is pain that makes us less arrogant, less superficial and less smug and with a greater sense of self-knowledge. An old saying reminds us that the olive needs to be crushed to reveal its true essence-the oil

F. Biography Versus the Novel

Given the public's high interest in celebrity media, biography and autobiography have replaced the novel. One reason biography has risen to the forefront of popular interest is because biographers in the last half of the twentieth century have wedded good historical research and narrative strategy with creative storytelling techniques found in solid novels.

Some of this sea change has come from the growing interest in historical narrative, and narrative theology, which argues that history should be written as story, rather than history as sociology or statistics. The reality is that this may only be half-true. In any case, many historians like the late Barbara Tuchman, the Pulitzer Prize winner Doris Kearns Goodwin and Stephen Ambrose have written their biographies in such a way as to keep the reader turning the pages to find out what happens next.

1. Similarity Between Biography and the Novel

The time-honored goal of the novelist has been to tell a story of how men and women lived in a given society and how they were affected by one another and by their environment. Novels are stories about the lives of everyday people doing their normal everyday activities. *Jane Eyre* and *Wuthering Heights* by Emily and Charlotte Bronte are prime examples of this fact. The task of the novelist is to create an environment for the reader in which the characters come alive and the reader feels as if they are actually meeting the subjects and are visiting and living in the same geographical places as the characters. This not only creates a story that gives the reader pleasure, but the novel also communicates serious knowledge about the past social, environmental and spiritual conditions.

And this is precisely what the biographer needs to do as well. However, the difference between a novel and a biography is that in a novel the novelist can arbitrarily place the main character in a physical, emotional or spiritual situation where he or she is uncomfortable or is in a place of danger or conflict. The biographer, on the other hand, must not violate the rules of accuracy and honesty. Unlike the novelist who can invent the obstacles and adventures that must be overcome, the biographer finds them through factual interviews and research.[1]

Part of the drama in the story of the two young people carrying on a long-distance romance centered around the clashes, misunderstandings,

---

1 Solid research gives the biographer insight, authority and confidence that strengthen the story.

and conflicts they experienced in an effort to learn how to relate to one another. When I read their letters and diaries I concluded their story had all the elements of a grand romantic novel. Here was a young woman passionately in love with one man who after many struggles and vicissitudes and after overcoming seemingly insurmountable odds finally married the man of her dreams. While this story had all the elements of a fictional novel, the reality was that it was a factual and true biography.

2. Writing History as A Narrative

Both the novelist and the biographer have a similar task. Namely, to infuse their story with as much drama and suspense as possible. Therefore, the biographer takes the pieces of an individual's life and re-assembles them into a story with a beginning, middle and ending. This can mean using fictional devices like flashback to establish and illuminate the character's history. The object is to show the action rather than to tell what the character did. As in a novel, so too in biography, I try to get the reader emotionally hooked within the first several paragraphs. Early in the story I want the reader to know there are problems and challenges the hero must try to overcome. The novelist does the same. I also try to create empathy and identification between the reader and the main character by using dialogue and showing action that reveals individual character. As in a novel, the reader of a biography should truly care what happens to the hero of the story, and in many cases feel a sense of loss when the story has ended.

3. Does Writing History as Narrative Violate the Scientific Presentation of Evidence?

Earlier I said the nature of story should arouse curiosity and compel the reader to keep turning the pages of the book to discover what happens next. However, having made such a statement, I suspect there are some in academia who object and say such a notion is against the "rules" of scholarship and historical research. My only defense to is to say that I have yet to meet a totally objective, impersonal and dispassionate scientist or historian. In the writing of science, history and biography, as in a novel, the author must, by the nature of his or her humanity, make interpretive judgment, about a person's character, motives and moral choices. Storytelling involves emphasizing some anecdotes and subordinating others, highlighting some facts and ignoring others. Storytelling and scientific investigation both require recording the ineffectiveness of one experiment and the success of another. The scientist and the biographer both look for hidden meaning in the facts they have assembled. Both must use their imaginative skills to fill blanks in the narrative. However, before scientists or biographers can, with integrity, interpret a life imaginatively they must have thoroughly steeped themselves in the data, facts and every bit of information that can be accumulated about their subject. To be effective in their discipline scientists and authors must make selections, shape detail and be aware of the audience. Above all, the author or scientist must have developed a carefully focused thesis that, for better or worse, makes a specific point of view. All of which should come out of the writer's cogitation, experience, research, passion and imagination.

G. The Mission Story

Since I have used the word "imagination" in relationship to the artistry of nonfiction, I need to say a word about why some editors are less than interested in publishing mission or cross-cultural stories. A universal complaint among many of the publishers and editors I have known is:

Too many nonfiction biographies are like diaries--dry and lifeless. They simply recount events and offer little to interest the reader.

When I first began to write one editor said, "Let me give you a tip about how to publish mission-related books." With a wry smile and upturned brow, he said, "I want to read about the missionary who yelled at his kids and kicked the dog under the table."

A bit of hyperbole to be sure, but the point the editor wanted me to understand was that readers need to identify with the main character. Aristotle said characters in literature that move us deeply are *People like ourselves.* The reality is that most people do not like, or cannot relate to "saints." Years later the words of that editor came to mind one evening after viewing the premiere showing of a missionary film. The film told the story of two women translators in Colombia who had lived in a high cold mountain village without running water, heat or electricity and with the constant threat of terrorists. In reality the most difficult task the translators faced was learning an extremely difficult language when they were middle-aged and doing battle mentally and spiritually to bring about the completion of a New Testament.

As I exited the auditorium I overheard two women discussing the film. "That was an interesting story," said one woman, "But I couldn't relate to the translators, they were just too holy for me." While I could not deny the woman her feelings I thought this was a mistaken interpretation of the film. Most cross-cultural workers I know are only too aware of their humanity and vulnerability. Knowing this, how can a biographer write about the triumph of the human spirit in a way that will not appear to the average reader to be overly spiritual or maudlin? I think part of the answer is found in Scripture where we find God using flawed characters, which in spite of themselves bring about His will. Writers of the Hebrew Scriptures were unafraid to deny the dysfunctions and failures of their heroes to posterity.

H.   Balance of Forces

The term "balance of forces" in story has to do with a change of tempo in the story that acts as a kind of breather, or a time out. While story hinges upon the character's struggle with external physical forces or internal ideas and conflicts, there must be time when the subject is relaxed and allowed to reflect on what is occurring in his or her life. In his book, *Adrift Seventy-Six Days Lost at Sea,* Steven Callahan could easily have overwhelmed the reader with the despair and utter hopelessness of being cast adrift in the middle of the Pacific Ocean in a rubber life raft without water or food for seventy-six days. Yet in the midst of this life-and-death struggle, Callahan gives the reader a variety of "breathers" with flashbacks about his earlier life: sailing, a failed marriage and a boat race in the company of a lovely young woman who found him to be all business and no romance. Callahan knew that story is more than high action sequences. He purposely gave the reader intervals when there was some comic relief. One such device was to call his raft *Rubber Ducky.*

When I say that story is more than a series of high action sequences I am not taking away from my major point that story must have conflict and action. That remains true. However, if all you have are a series of actions and conflicts that are unrelated to a story line, then all you have is a series of episodes, or raw story material, and this is not story. A story needs a plot structure. That is, the reader should know the action is leading to some kind of conclusion and resolution. In my books on Cameron Townsend I tried to balance the high dramatic moments with moments when he was able to enjoy his favorite dessert—cherry pie. There were scenes when the president of Mexico, Lázaro Cárdenas came to visit Townsend to discuss the heavy burden he carried about having to incur the disfavor of the United States over Mexico's decision to expropriate foreign oil. There were other times when the president dismissed his aides and the two men talked on the back porch of the Townsend village house as friend to friend. There were moments when Townsend went swimming, played tennis and took a morning stroll beside a lake. These were the relief moments between the peak action scenes that allowed both the character and the reader to examine calmly what was happening in his life's journey.

I.   Place/Setting

Next to knowing how to write about people, you should know how to write about place. People and places are the twin pillars on which most nonfiction is built. Every human event happens somewhere, and the reader wants to know what that "somewhere" was like.[1]

This quote from William Zinsser's book *On Writing Well* is an excellent example of what I mean by the importance of place or setting in your prose. Some people think of place or setting as merely a perfunctory backdrop to the main story. This may be true for some stories, but place, with its topography, scenery and climate can often become one of the central characters in a story. My book *Good Broth to Warm Our Bones* is set against the harsh climate of Barrow, Alaska in the 1950s. As the story unfolds it becomes clear the arctic weather defines the events and actions of the characters. On more than one occasion, the extreme cold, ice and snow become the villain over which the protagonist does battle.

Setting or place can also become a metaphor for something akin to spiritual values. Names like Norman Rockwell, Currier and Ives and Thomas Kinkade spring to mind as examples of people whose pastoral

---

1   William Zinsser, *On Writing Well, An Informal Guide to Writing Nonfiction*, (New York: Harper & Row Publishers, 1980), p. 4.

background settings in art generate an inner longing and way of life and moment in time that suggests peace and tranquility. If a writer like Jan Karon (*At Home in Mitford* series) sets his or her story in a "quiet Midwestern town," this has a different connotation than if the story is set in New York, Los Angeles, Hollywood or Las Vegas. These are, of course, stereotypical settings and a biographer must deal with the reality that a story set in Las Vegas might defy its stereotype. Stories set at a particular season of the year like, *A Christmas Carol* or in a specific historical period like *A Tale of Two Cities*, which takes place during the French Revolution, are as important to the story as are the characters Charles Dickens created.

J.   Why I Write Biography

One reason why I am drawn to biography as story is because I believe stories of real people contain more unusual and colorful adventures, facts, traits, idiosyncrasies and story ideas than any one person might dream of on their own. Biography invites the reader to examine real people responding to their world, that in turn allows us to see the effects and changes they brought to the place and era in which they lived. This may be one reason why in the last half of the twentieth century, nonfiction books, which includes biography, have displaced novels as the most widely read and influential books on many publishers' lists. My further interest in biography as story has to do with a fundamental belief that reading books of literary value and of stories about the higher virtues of love, self-sacrifice devotion, servanthood, caring, compassion etc., can help shape one's moral vision.

Some might argue that this is too large a role for art and story to assume. While I am without statistical proof, it is my personal belief that great works of art, music and story can and do play a decisive role in changing and creating a more civilized society. This was the goal of Johann Sebastian Bach's organ music. Bach wrote and played his music for the greater glory of God. As such he wanted it to move people to something altogether bigger than personal emotion. He wanted his music to take you out of yourself. Robert Wuthnow helps us to see this idea more clearly when he writes:

If the Good Samaritan story were to drop out of our culture, something vital would be lost.[1]

In his book *Anthills of the Savannah*, African author Chinua Achebe wrote:

A wise old man insists that storytelling is more important to a community than drumming or fighting a war. Why is this so? Because it is only story that outlives the sound of war-drums and the exploits of brave fighters. It is story that saves our progeny from blundering like blind beggars into spikes of the cactus fence. The story is our escort. Without it we are blind. Does the blind man own his escort? No, neither do we the story, rather it is the story that owns and directs us.[2] Such is the nature of story.

1   Robert Wuthnow, *Acts of Compassion* (Princeton, New Jersey: Princeton University Press, 1991), p. 159 ff, 179.
2   *Context*, Chicago, (Volume 18, Number 15, November 15, 1996), p. 6.

Chapter Two
The Creative Attitude, Part I

A. What is Creativity?

Most people recognize it when they see, hear, feel or in other ways encounter that quintessential experience we call creativity. Yet there is a certain puzzlement about how creativity happens. Stewart Bronfeld, a longtime producer/writer for NBC, echoes what I have come to believe about the nature of creativity when he says:

> The magic of the creative process remains basically mysterious, like any other kind of birth. The art is a product of the artist's personality and thus differs with each person. But the craft requires experience, common sense and professional techniques and can be learned and practiced.[1]

Clearly individual creativity is infinitely varied. How a person sets a dinner table, carves a sinuous dolphin out of soapstone, restores a vintage automobile, writes a novel, teaches a responsive third grade class-- all require creativity. Yet people we consider highly creative in their dis-

---

1 Stewart Bonfeld, Creating Television Stories and Characters, (Boston, *The Writer*, October, 1991), p.15.

cipline are often unable to explain their own creative processes question of how he conceived of his many innovative and creative ideas.

Cameron Townsend, founder of Wycliffe Bible Translators and one of the great mission statesmen of the twentieth century, was never able to answer the question of where his ideas came from.

Curiously, there is a continuing debate among psychologists, who specialize in human development and education, on two fundamental premises about creativity. One school holds that creativity is a skill that can, and should, be taught and encouraged. The other says the culture can only tolerate a handful of creative people in each generation. This school believes, for example, that industry will generate far more ideas than it can realistically use. Thus, reality puts a boundary on what industries, or other disciplines, believe is needed and useful. One of my schoolteacher daughters is particularly sympathetic to this notion because she says it is extremely difficult to handle twenty-five or thirty highly original creative third graders. Thus, most pumpkins and turkeys are drawn and colored (inside the lines) with relative uniformity.

1. Creativity is an Inherent Gift

For the record, I believe creativity is an inherent gift given to us by the Creator. Just as it's in our genes as a species to be musical, so too, I believe, we humans have a built-in capacity to be creative to one degree or another.

When I think of creativity I think of the amazing diversity God gave us in creation. Because I believe men and women are made in the image of God, we humans are called to think God's thoughts after Him. This gives men and women incredible freedom and impetus to explore their creative impulses.

Yet not everyone feels free to vent these impulses. One reason for this has to do with pressure from peers, educators and society at large to conform to the status quo. The second reason in the case of would-be writers has to do with becoming saturated with rules, regulations and the mechanics of grammatical construction.

I once went through a period in my writing career when I read everything Northrop Frye had published on Literary Criticism. I had written many articles and half a dozen books, but during that time when I tried to think creatively about crafting an article or beginning a new book I felt I was experiencing something akin to stage fright. I later concluded my creative energies were being stifled because I was overwhelmed with left-brain logic. I was so afraid of making a literary mistake that my subjective creativity was being undermined and overwhelmed. I escaped my dilemma by some words from Wendell Johnson, who said:

> One may learn how to write with mechanical correctness [but] one may still have to learn how to write with significance and validity. As long as the student's primary anxieties revolve around the rules of syntax, spellings, [etc.,] he [or she] is not likely to communicate effectively.[1]

Literary Criticism still remains an interest for me, but I now read such material only when I am not in a subjective writing posture.

2. The "Aha" Moment

After probing into the so-called mystery of creativity, I have discovered some clues, or patterns, that when followed lead to interesting and satisfying conclusions about the nature of creativity. Some of the patterns include a repetition or replay of the same sequence of events projected over time-sometimes a long time. Other patterns include giving your subconscious mind a problem and then engaging in playful relaxation that can include a walk, listening to music, going to a good movie or play, cooking a meal, anything that allows an emotional discharge from the pressure of trying to forcibly solve the problem. Sports psychologists often encourage professional and Olympic athletes to take time away from their game or training as a way to relieve performance anxiety and freshen their perspective. Also, part of the mystery surrounding creativity seems to occur when an individual suddenly has that "aha" moment, that whack on the head, that insight that gives a solution to a long-standing or vexing problem. Newton and the apple fit this scenario.

---

1   Edited by S.I. Hayakawa, *The Use and Misuse of Language*, (New York, A Fawcett World Library, 1958) Pp.102,103.

3. Creativity Requires More than Just Desire

I have deliberately used the word creative "attitude" because I believe creativity is released from deep within individuals only when they are fully present to, and inwardly aware of the problem they are trying to solve. Fundamentally, writing is problem solving. How will you define your character? Where and when should you begin the story? What research should you use and when and how should you end the story? Such problems need to be addressed creatively.

To say it another way, creative energy takes place, not just by having a casual desire. Rather, it occurs when a person gives serious attention and discipline to whatever project or problem they want to solve. For this to happen, a writer's state of mind must be open to growth and new ideas. People searching for creative solutions to a problem usually have such words as pro-active, passion and desire, ascribed to them.

4. Passion

One of my favorite words to describe the creative attitude is passion. Boris Pasternak (author of Dr. Zhivago) in his autobiography says it is passion that must guide the eye of the poet. He also says that writers should have the passion of creative contemplation. When I talk about passion, I mean the human hopes, aspirations, doubts, loves, hates, and the glory of beauty that one finds in the finest of English literature, in nature and in the human comedy. In his book, Søren Kierkegaard's Christian Psychology. C. Stephen Evans helps us understand passion in a fuller way when he says:

> Passion [is] a key term in Kierkegaard's writings. Passion is not merely a momentary feeling, an external force that sweeps a person out of control, as "he shot her in a fit of passion." Such momentary emotions are purely aesthetic for Kierkegaard. The truly significant passions are those enduring concerns that give shape and unity to a person's life. The distinction between the aesthetic and the ethical life is that the ethical person has begun to develop some passions, which are more than the momentary

impulses that shape the aesthete. The ethical person cares about such things as kindness, gratitude, fairness and fidelity.[1]

It is such passions as these that fuel the writer with perseverance to keep probing for solutions and fresh possibilities. I believe it is this regular discipline of sitting down each day in front of your computer and writing when you feel like it and when you feel absolutely devoid of any original ideas. The curious paradox about creativity in writing is that an idea for a story can occur in an instant. Paul Gallico wrote a charming love story called *The Enchanted Doll* when he happened to spot a lovely hand-painted doll in a shop window in England. The idea for the story was instantaneous, but the working out of that idea required the investment of time, energy, research and hard work. Creativity and inspiration never come out of nothing. Rather they come out of good solid research.

B. Definitions

In an attempt to demystify the complexity of creativity I consulted my CD-ROM dictionary. From more than thirty definitions I discovered only two that I resonated with. One was:

1. To Make Visible

And this, I suggest, will be one of the major themes of this book. I have a fundamental belief that most people are more gifted and talented than they might believe themselves to be. Further, I believe one's particular worldview, experience and uniqueness can bring a texture and insight to a particular piece of literature that no other writer can. Additionally, you may be the only person with a vision and passion to bring a particular story to light. Sally E. Stuart says very much the same thing in the introduction to her book *Christian Writers' Market Guide* when she says:

> We often feel inadequate to the task, but I learned a long time ago the writing assignments God has given me couldn't be written quite as well by anyone else.

---

1   C. Stephen Evans, *Soren Kierkegaard's Christian Psychology*, (Grand Rapids, Michigan, Zondervan Publishing House, 1990), p. 18.

The parable of the shepherd who leaves the ninety and nine sheep to search out the one sheep that was lost is a powerful metaphor that shows how God loves and values our individual uniqueness and worth. At the end of the day, society usually looks at humans pragmatically. The bottom line question industry asks is, "What is a person's utilitarian value?" Not so with God. The Scriptures tell us that the Good Shepherd knows each sheep individually and calls it by name. But the question remains, what clues are there to help you decide if you are the one to write a particular story?

One simple clue might be a desire. If you have an itch or a desire to write about a person who, in your opinion and the opinion of a larger community, is an example of a life that affirms and acknowledge the value of what is good, true and honest, then perhaps this is a story you should write. If you don't, that important life history may never be written. It is through story, after all, that imaginations are enlarged and moral absolutes appropriated to become part of one's life

2. Car Lights at Night:

The second definition that attempted to define creativity was Creativity is like driving a car at night. You never see further than your headlights, but you can make the trip that way. The research on a four-volume biography on the life and times of William Cameron Townsend, founder of Wycliffe Bible Translators required that I read through over 40,000 pieces of literature, letters, diaries and other documents (25,000 for Volume Four alone). If I had thought about reading that material all in one great gulp, I would have collapsed. But little by little, as I took one small step at a time, the creative juices illuminated the road with just enough light to write one chapter at a time, and that kept me from becoming overwhelmed.

3. My Personal Definition of Creativity

My own definition of creativity is that it is a little like being in love. When your are in love, you have a passion to be sensitive to another, to break away from yourself, to see life from the viewpoint of the one with whom you are in love. Your world has always been there, but you now begin to see it in a new light, from a new angle, you are even willing to entertain and explore new ideas and to take risks. In a way you are seeing everything for the first time in its original freshness.

4. Being in Love with God

Being in love with God can also increase creativity and give one a new perspective on life. In my book, *They Dared to be Different*, Mariano, the principal character, talks about his personal encounter with God:

> When I was in the presence of sin, I did not think whether the day was nice or not. It was just a day. I looked at the mountains, the caves, the river, but not once did I draw into myself whether it was beautiful or not.

> Now that I am a believer, I experience the freedom that comes through our Lord Jesus Christ. I see wonder, I see beauty, I feel it. Every day that passes has meaning. I go for a walk and I enjoy God's beauty. I even hear things I never heard before.

One afternoon several years later after Mariano told me that, and more than three thousand miles from Mexico, I sat on a log beside a small river deep in the Brazilian jungle with a man named Servo. When I asked Servo what his life was like now that he was a believer in Jesus Christ, his words were remarkably similar to those of Mariano's:

> Before I stood up to become a follower of Jesus, I walked through the jungle and did not notice that the trees and sky were pretty. When I saw a bird I thought only of killing it. Nothing around me seemed beautiful. Now because I know the Maker of all things, I look around and enjoy all the things God has made. Flowers now are food for my eyes.[1]

It was Servo who taught me to look at the different shades of green in the jungle.

C.   Openness to New Experiences

1   Hugh Steven, *To The Ends of the Earth*, (Huntington Beach, California, Wycliffe Bible Translators, Inc. 1986), p. 80.

I want to underscore some words that keep popping up in this discussion of creativity. They are words like *spontaneity, thinking* (i.e., the process of *reflective thinking), sensitivity and breaking away from the usual sequences of thought.* Readers of the Gospels in the New Testament know that one of the essential characteristics of Jesus' ministry was to challenge the status quo. Jesus continually urged his disciples to look for deeper meaning in his words and actions (read John, Chapter 7 as an example.) Jesus willingness to eat a social meal with outcasts, his controversial healing ministry that included his gift of physically touching lepers, the so-called triumphal entry into Jerusalem and the temple cleansing are actions that are greater than the sum of their parts. When we read these accounts, we are asked to consider and apply the story's principles and deeper meaning to our lives.

1. Parables on Food and Farming

Interestingly, more than half of Jesus' parables in the New Testament are about food, feasts or farming. What might the deeper meaning of these parables be? Since parables are usually open-ended, I can think of many applications, but two stand out in my mind.

a. The Place of the Home

One is the place of the home. I think of my home as a citadel, a place of refuge, comfort and security for my wife, family and friends against a hostile world.

b. Eating Together

The second is the importance of eating together as a family. When we eat a meal together with friends and family, the table becomes a place of intimacy, a place for communion and celebration where our souls, as well as our bodies, are nourished. In this way we are reminded of the link between our family meal and Holy Communion. The lesson or the deeper truth is that we develop a sacramental view of life and the common joys of home, family and friendships.

The nature of our Christian faith encourages the creative celebration of special days and festivals. Our faith reminds us that home and hearth are to be guarded and held sacred. We are also challenged to accept others in the body with the same grace and love that has been given to us by God. I love the comment by C.S. Lewis who, when describing the affinity he had with the "Inklings" (Tolkien, Charles Williams, Nevil Coghill the Chaucer scholar, and others), said:

> We meet on Friday evenings in my rooms. What I owe to them is incalculable. Is any pleasure on earth as great as a circle of Christian friends by a good fire? [1]

Lewis's Narnia series and Tolkien's Hobbit stories, reflect the theme of hearth, home and good fellowship around a cozy fire with "cups of tea and cakes, tankards of beer and thick sandwiches, pipes, and hot baths" that emerge with regularity. These men celebrated the sheer pleasure of good tastes, the goodness of creation, the smells and texture of fresh bread, raspberries, nuts and even the lowly bean that Lewis lauds in a poem.[2]

D. Crossing Over Pre-Ordained Boundaries

What is it about the creative person that sets him or her apart from the herd? Certainly creative people are observant. They notice how different people walk and talk and what their body language communicates. The late Sir Alec Guinness said:

> I try to get inside a character and project him. One of my own private rules of thumb is that I have not got a character until I have mastered exactly how he walks.

Creative people are aware of sights, sounds and smells. The smell of warm earth after a summer rain. The sounds of homecoming, a grumpy foghorn on a mist-covered seashore and feelings that a train whistles evokes in one's memory. Yet as necessary as it is to be sensitive to aesthetic stimuli and to translate that emotion into prose, I believe there is a more fundamental attitude for the creative person to develop, namely, to be open to the possibility of new experiences.

---

1   William Ready, *Understanding Tolkien and Lord of the Rings*, (New York, Warner Press, 1973), p. 25.
2   Thomas Howard, *C.S. Lewis. Man of Letters*, (San Francisco, Ignatius Press, 1987), p. 55.

Creative people generally like to investigate the nature of things. Such an attitude requires an open-mindedness, a playfulness, a curiosity and desire to explore new ideas and to dream of new possibilities. One of the hallmarks of a good writer is his or her desire to acquire new information and to give that information away in their writing. However, in some cases, the exploration of new ideas and new information may be culturally uncomfortable and defy accepted societal logic.

E   . Move Beyond the Established Order

The great social reformers of history who worked hard against entrenched political and religious power and privilege would certainly qualify as examples of those who moved beyond the established order. Jesus, of course, is a prime example of one who defied the societal logic of his day. Jesus began his public ministry with a series of dramatic events that could only be described as a conflict between him and the authority of the scribal establishment. One might say that Jesus was involved in social criticism when he challenged and overturned the moneychangers in the Temple. And certainly he did the same when he challenged the Scribes or the Pharisees who were committed to the status quo.

F. Openness to New Possibilities

Thus one of the most striking characteristics of a creative person is the willingness to move beyond the established order and to be open to new possibilities. Savvy business executives who are competing in the rapidly changing global market want employees who can "break away from old attitudes and are willing to adapt to new realities." One executive writing in *Time* magazine said. "As we enter the twenty-first century we want to engender a frontier spirit in our work force." The interesting thing to note about this attitude is that it is a major shift in emphasis. In the past, industry was more concerned with the creative development and production of things and ideas and less interested in developing and encouraging creative people. While this attitude may seem to be right out of the Year-2000 handbook, Wycliffe founder, William Cameron Townsend, fostered the ideas and concept of pioneering in the early 1930s. And before that, Alexander Graham Bell said:

Don't keep forever on the public road, going only where others have gone. Leave the beaten track occasionally and dive into the woods. You will be certain to find something you have never seen before. It will be a little thing, but don't ignore it. One discovery will lead to another, and before you know it, you will have something worth thinking and (writing) about.

G. What Does a Creative Writer Need?

Phil Cousineau in his book *The Art of the Pilgrimage* said:

What matters most on your journey is how deeply you see, how attentively you hear, how richly the encounters are felt in your heart and soul[1]

1. Rediscovery of the Common

The creative writer also needs an ability to rediscover the beauty in common details. If you take an apple and cut it from pole to pole, nothing of significance shows up on the two halves. However, if you cut the apple around the circumference, you will discover a lovely star burst design. This simple experiment illustrates the importance of standing an idea on its head and looking at a problem from a different angle. It also illustrates the importance of rediscovering the things around us that we take for granted, or have grown accustomed to.

When was the last time you really examined the leaves on a tree, the tree itself, and the grain and texture of the bark of that tree. What about the color of the sky before a storm? Have you stopped to smell fir trees in the sun, or looked deeply into the face of someone you love? Have you noticed the gleam of shiny furniture, or the skillfully woven pattern in a carpet that you walk over each day? The difference between creative people and less creative people seems to be this ability to pay attention or to see things and ideas that others miss, and then to take their small ideas, play with them and turn them into bigger ideas. After all, ideas are useless unless people act on them.

2. Agatha Christie

1   Phil Cousineau, *The Art of the Pilgrimage*, (Berkeley California, Conakry Press, 1998), p. XXXIX.

Agatha Christie was one who knew how to see beauty and meaning in the ordinary. One of her interesting idiosyncrasies was that of eating a fresh peach on her best family-heirloom dessert plates. This is how she described those dessert plates:

> The edges were bright green, scalloped with gold, and in the center of each plate was a different fruit. My favorite was then, and always has been, the fig, a large juicy-looking purple fig.

3. Stumbling Over Discoveries

Winston Churchill said, "Men stumble over discoveries, but most pick themselves up and walk away." The creative cook is one who is able to recognize and capitalize on accidental combinations of ingredients.

a. Automobile Safety Glass

The first Triplex safety glass for automobiles windshields was used first by Henry Ford in 1927. It was invented by a French scientist who accidentally knocked a beaker onto the floor that contained a certain chemical resin. When the beaker fell, the scientist noticed that it simply cracked but didn't shatter. In time this led to the discovery of the auto safety windshield.

b. Alexander Graham Bell and Charles Goodyear

The famous splash of acid on Alexander Graham Bell's pants marks almost the exact moment the telephone was invented. And the clumsy spill of gum rubber and sulfur on a hot stove allowed Charles Goodyear to understand how to vulcanize rubber.

c. Clarence Birdseye

In 1916 on a fur-trading trip to Labrador with his wife and child, Clarence Birdseye was given some fish that had been quick-frozen in the frigid air, then thawed and cooked months later. Birdseye observed that fish, as well as the vegetables that had also been frozen in barrels of water and thawed, tasted remarkably fresh. Because of his keen observation (there's that word again) of a routine procedure, Birdseye launched the frozen food industry. (He had been working for U.S. The Geographic Society.) Industry, visual arts, literature, music, as well as science, philosophy, and even sports, are filled with examples of people who encountered or conceived two or more antitheses simultaneously, and often in apparent defiance of logic or physical possibility created something new.

H. David Milliken

David Milliken, one of Australia's leading commentators on theology and the arts said:

> It's a primal irritation that compels us to embark for our soul's life on the impossible task of creating another Eden through the aesthetic magic of the imagination. Fundamentally we are creative. Indeed I believe a very basic purpose of life is perpetual creativity. If we are followers of Christ, then I cannot see how it can be otherwise. Christ has opened up the eternal possibility of a new life, joy and beauty. It is Christ who has transformed our tentative acts of creativity to things of eternal significance. All else may fade away, but then things of beauty in this world will endure throughout eternity. For as we cooperate with him as agents of joy, beauty and the new life, we join with him in the preparation for paradise.[1]

---

1 I regret not being able to give the source for this quote. I use it because it resonates so powerfully with my own long-held belief about the nature of creativity.

Chapter Three

The Creative Attitude, Part II

New Ideas from Old and Knowing Who You Are Not

A. Johann Gutenberg (1397-1468)

The story of the German printer, Johann Gutenberg illustrates how, by nurturing a creative attitude one can discover new ideas from old realities. In the 1400s printing was used only to reproduce pictures, playing cards, designs on cloth and similar items. The designs were cut into wood blocks, stone or metal and transferred to parchment or vellum. Sometimes a few words of explanation were cut into the printing block, but that was the limit of text printing.

In the 1400s, Johann Gutenberg had, what seemed then to be, an impossible dream. He wanted to print whole pages of the Bible, but Gutenberg had a singular problem, how could one carve over 1300 pages of text onto wooden blocks? As he toyed with this dilemma, Gutenberg began to think about how coins were cast and the impression of seals in sealing wax. Then one day Gutenberg took part in a wine harvest and noticed the power of the wine press. From that observation, Gutenberg found the answer to his problem. He invented the letter press by combining the separate skills of stamping with a seal and pressing wine with a wine press. While hundreds before him had seen this, no one in Europe had observed or connected the two methods. The reason: he was probably the only person who was thinking about how to solve a problem and improve the way books and pamphlets were printed. Most, with the exception of Gutenberg, were satisfied with the status quo.

B. Making Something New Out of Something Old

This story illustrates the evolution of ideas in art, music, literature and industry usually comes from bits and pieces of information taken from a variety of sources and melded to make something new. It also illustrates, that far from being orderly, many of the world's major inventions would not be with us unless the scientist kept tripping, fumbling and then noticing what was happening. Admittedly, this is an abridged version of the Gutenberg story. The whole story of how he designed and built the first commercially effective printing facility is much larger and more complex than what I have given here.

1. What it means to have a creative attitude

The story of Gutenberg is a classic example of what I mean by having a creative attitude. First, Gutenberg was confronted with a problem he couldn't solve. The problem came from watching his father's drudging work as a scribe working in dim light with painstaking slowness copying books for the church and wealthy patrons. While Gutenberg admired his father's craftsmanship, he was more concerned with how he could, by some means, produce hundreds of beautiful pages of text in the time it took his father to produce just one.

2. Looking for a second answer

This tells us that people are more likely to respond creatively if they have been thinking and allowing their subconscious mind to play with the problem they are trying to solve. Note that the creativity I am talking about is not an act of creation in the sense of what God did in the

Old Testament by creating something out of nothing. The creativity I am talking about requires one to uncover, select, reshuffle, and synthesize already existing facts and ideas.

3. Eero Saarinen

Essentially, creativity is an act of discovery and a collision of seemingly unrelated ideas or facts. Sometimes people can find creative inspiration from the most mundane things. In 1956, architect Eero Saarinen was commissioned to design a building for TWA at what is now New York's Kennedy Airport. He struggled with a couple of designs, none of which he liked. Then one morning at breakfast he found himself staring at the curved shell of a grapefruit. Saarinen turned it over and began carving arches in it. He took the finished product to work, and added it to the other models involved in the final design. When the terminal was completed, it was described by an architectural magazine as, "A totality of fluid-form curving and circling within itself." The article never mentioned the grapefruit.

4. Turn an idea on its head

Creativity consists of seeing what everyone else has seen, but going one step beyond and thinking what nobody else has thought. It is being dissatisfied with what one sees and turning an idea on its head. C.S. Lewis did this brilliantly in *The Screwtape Letters* where he created the characters of a senior devil Screwtape who writes a series of letters to Wormwood, a junior devil on how to beguile and corrupt people of Christian faith.

5. The itch of creativity

The creative process has often been defined as a kind of itch, a surging inner tension, a yearning, a hunch, even confused excitement. In 1871 after a three-month trip down the Mississippi to New Orleans from his home in Kentucky, John James Audubon wrote in his diary that he was now ready to fulfill "My ardent wish ever since boyhood to draw a complete collection of the birds of our country from nature, all of natural size."

C. Relaxation Equals Incubation

Proverbs. 14:30, (LB) says, "A relaxed attitude lengthens a man's life; jealousy rots it away." This may sound like a contradiction, or even counterproductive, but part of the creative process involves the ability to relax and play. Problem solving, it seems, is most likely to occur when a person's mind is relaxed, receptive and doing something else. Standing too close to one's work for too long can actual impede one's judgment. The "aha" moment for Gutenberg came when he wasn't sitting at his desk pumping his brain to find the answer to his problem. Rather, he was relaxed in the receptive atmosphere of a wine festival. Gutenberg had, however, given his subconscious mind an assignment. With the logical part of his brain at rest, the ideas Gutenberg had for solving his problem were simmering and incubating in the creative part of his brain. Admittedly this is not a sophisticated explanation of the nature of creativity. But the history of where and when people got their fresh ideas and creative insights and breakthroughs seem to have come during moments of relaxation after there had been a period of incubation.

1. Mozart

It's interesting that Mozart got the idea for the melody of the "Magic Flute" quintet while playing billiards.

2. Dr. Frederick Grant Banting

Frederick Banting was a young struggling Canadian surgeon who he had to teach to make a living. One October night in 1920, Banting was going over his next day's lecture. His subject was diabetes. Hour after hour he poured over the literature of this dread disease. Finally, with his head whirling with a maze of conflicting theories, case histories and accounts of experiments with dogs, he went to bed. At two a.m., Banting suddenly woke up, turned on the light and wrote three sentences in his notebook. *Tie off pancreatic duct of dogs. Wait six to eight weeks for degeneration. Remove residue and extract.* He then went back to bed and slept. Those three magic sentences led to the discovery of insulin. Banting's conscious mind came to grips with one of the most baffling problems in medical science. His subconscious mind finished the job.

D. The Subconscious Mind

Many psychologists and people who study the process of conscious thought believe creativity depends largely on one's use of the subconscious mind. One of the unique aspects of the so-called subconscious mind is that we can't pump or force it to work. This section of our brain that has all our accumulated wisdom and experience is waiting to help us when we stop taking ourselves too seriously.

1. Dr. J. B. Rhine

Having made a case for the use of the subconscious, I need to say that not everyone agrees with this notion. Dr. J.B. Rhine, former director of *Parapsychology* (the study of phenomena that can't be explained by scientific or empirical evidence) at Duke University, has a problem with the notion that one should try to develop one's subconscious mind. Rather, he says:

> I am convinced that our most creative thinking can be done best in more relaxed and spontaneous states of mind. I would accent, therefore, fresh and unstained thinking, more than subconscious itself.

E. Prayer, Play and Mediation

The University of Northern Colorado did a study that evaluated the dynamic relationship between play (in which an individual loses himself in joyful recreation that stimulates energies and gives zest for living) and prayer or meditation (which replenishes an individual's spirit and restores perspective on the business of living). The study concluded that students did better and more productive work when they included these elements as part of their life-style. *Psychology Today* published similar findings in an article entitled *The Power of Play.*

[Play] refreshes us and recharges us. It restores our optimism. It changes our perspective, stimulating creativity. It renews our ability to accomplish the work of the world.[1]

1. Lewis Sperry Chafer

Lewis Sperry Chafer, founder of Dallas Theological Seminary, once reminded a young workaholic, Cameron Townsend, founder of Wycliffe Bible Translators, that he could do more work in eleven months than he could in twelve.

F. Creativity Operates on More than One Plane

An interesting fact to remember about creativity is that while routine thinking takes place on only one plane, the creative act takes place on more than one level.

1. Picasso

A story about Picasso's early childhood helps us understand how this works. As a schoolboy, Picasso was terrible at math. Whenever the teacher wrote the number 4 on the blackboard, it looked like a nose to him and he kept doodling to fill in the rest of the face. Everyone else in the class saw the number 4. Picasso perceived a face. Only in hindsight can we now appreciate the irony of that situation. Picasso, as it turned out, became one of the world's greatest artists.

G. A Price to Pay

However, there is often a price to pay when the creative person crosses over pre-ordained boundaries and questions convention. This was true for Picasso. He was unconventional and his teachers told him he would never amount to anything. Likewise Einstein, who found math puzzling and was considered by his early teachers to be a poor student, (Einstein wanted to understand concepts or reasons why behind his teacher's often autocratic statements.) Shortly before he died, a young student at Princeton asked Einstein what he thought was the most important attribute of the successful mind. Without hesitation, Einstein

1 Hara Estroff Marano, *The Power of Play*, (*Psychology Today*, New York, August, 1999), p. 17.

answered, *to have an insatiable curiosity and a driving spirit of inquiry.* However, such insatiability can sometimes set a person apart from the norm and make him or her suspect. At least that was the case with our friend Gutenberg.

1. Gutenberg

All his life, he struggled with poverty and fought against legal manipulators. When he spoke about his idea of producing hundreds of beautiful pages in the time it took his father to produce one, all without errors and deviations from copy to copy (deviations always appeared in scribes' work, no matter how painstaking they were), he was vilified by the scribes' guild. When he told his fellow printers they could work faster with movable type, the scribes thought they would lose their jobs and began spreading rumors that Gutenberg was an alchemist working on "devilish" things in his workshop. Gutenberg's answer to the skeptics and rumormongers was to draw the shades of his workshop and re-dedicate himself to his experiments. Thus, unconventional people can create a certain enmity and bitterness, or professional jealousy among their peers.

2. Erica Jong and C.S. Lewis

Erica Jong, author of *Fear of Flying* and five other novels and works of poetry, said:

> There is a strong cultural imperative in this society to make people (who are successful) self-destruct. You are allowed one big success and then they will try to kill you. But I am a spiritual enough person to know I can't let what the whole world thinks of me stop me from writing my book.

C.S. Lewis faced a similar hatred from his academic fellows at Magdalen College as well as those in the Oxford faculties of theology and English literature. This occurred when Lewis began to achieve worldwide recognition and success for his Narnia series and other writings.

3. Leveling

In Australia they talk about cutting off the heads of tall poppies. It's called "leveling, or knocking down the heads of nails that are sticking up." "The reason for such behavior," said Henry Clay, a great speaker of a past age, "is if you are successful at anything, those who aren't will be jealous."

To be your own man or woman is a hard, sometimes lonely, frightening prospect. Peer pressure to conform to the norm of your group can be one of the great destroyers of the creative spirit. The question then becomes, if this is true, how can a person exhibit the heroic virtues of courage, endurance, devotion, magnanimity and superiority of soul to circumstances? One answer is to know who you are and who you are not.

H. Knowing Who You Are Not

Knowing who you are not, is as important as knowing who you are. When I have an opportunity to meet young people who I sense are finding their identity in a herd mentality or who are being swept along by a current of peer pressure, I admit that belonging to a group is easier and more secure. I also add that conforming to peer pressure can leave them in a rut of mediocrity.

1. Rudyard Kipling

Rudyard Kipling once said, *No price is too high to pay* for *the privilege of owning yourself.* This truth has wide implications for the writer because it touches on an individual's core values, personal character, integrity and self-knowledge. How, for example do young people who are serious about practicing their Christian faith resist becoming entangled with the negative forces of their culture? It's not just the many "isms" that attack and want to reshape the church, so also do the more impersonal influences of the marketplace, or the forces associated with modernization. Accommodation to such forces is not always bad and some are necessary, but they can sometimes be dangerous and seductive. For example, those who consider it a mark of sophistication to be cynical and sneer at the person who expresses a desire to live and act according to biblical principles and Christian ethics is often excluded from the "loop."

However, having a settled conviction about who you are and who you are not, gives you an inner strength that enables you to resist those who try to influence you against your will. How many tragic stories there are of people who have been misguided by evil, or by sexual tensions that have led to personal disaster because they were not certain about their own identity.

2. John the Baptist, Martin Luther, the Apostle Paul and Jesus

Some interesting people in history who knew who they were and were not, were John the Baptist, Martin Luther, the Apostle Paul and, of course, Jesus. When people asked John the Baptist if he was the Christ, he, knowing who was not, said, *No I am not the Christ, I am a voice crying in the wilderness.* When Martin Luther nailed his 95 protests on the Wittenberg church door he, knowing who he was and what he believed, was able to challenge the most powerful man in Christendom, Pope Leo the Tenth. Leo had authorized the sale of indulgences to bolster his cash-strapped treasury.

As history tells us, Luther paid a steep price for his courage to challenge what he believed to be an unconscionable violation of Scripture. Yet he endured the pain because he knew when man's strength fails, God's strength begins. In one of his writings, Luther echoed the Apostle Paul's words:

> If humans embrace the cross, they may be scorned as spineless and foolish. But that is not the last word, for to embrace the cross is also to embrace the world as it actually is in its most essential reality. We come to know the mystery of God...Christ, in whom are hidden all the treasures of wisdom and knowledge.[1]

When Luther appeared at the Diet of Worms to give an account of his writings and was asked if he would recant, Luther, whose conscience was captive to the Word of God said:

---

1 Mark A. Noll, *Turning Points, Decisive Moments in the History of Christianity,* (Grand Rapids, Michigan, Baker Books, 1997), p. 170.

Unless I am bound and forced in my mind by arguments, which convey conviction to retract, it is not safe to do it. Here I am. I cannot! I dare not! I will not! So help me, God. Amen.[1]

In the opening verses of the first chapter of his letter to the Philippians the Apostle Paul, with a clear understanding of who he was said: I am here for the defense of the gospel (1:16). And Jesus, knowing who he was and where he was going, willingly assumed the posture of a slave, a servant and washed the feet of his disciples. This model of servant leadership and the new commandment, *that you love one another even as I have loved you,* is the legacy Jesus wanted to leave for all believers for all time. Knowing that He came to serve, not to be served, allowed Jesus the freedom to uniquely minister to people. Knowing that you are a personal representative of Christ on earth frees you from inflating your own ego and allows you the freedom to treat others with love, care and respect. Knowing you are a woman and not a man allows you to celebrate your femininity.

4. The Task of the Writer

If you are wondering what all this has to do with writing biography, the answer is, that it is pivotal. The task of the biographer is to explore the character and uniqueness of another human being. To do this with sensitivity and empathy the writer must have a right understanding of his or her core values. To be a writer takes courage, to honestly confront your subject as well as the courage to confront yourself. *The limit to which one has self-understanding is the limit to which you can understand others,* said my professor friend Jim Houston. He also said *"If we conceive the world to be a desert, we also make it such.*[2] Houston frequently reminded his students of the Augustinian prayer, *Let me know Thee, O God, and let me know myself.*

It is also fair to say that such a self-understanding does not always come full-blown. Discovering your core values and the priorities that are important to you takes time since it grows out of your own self-discovery. It may be that you know who you are, but not where you are going. Sometimes it helps to clarify your thinking to actually write your

1 Erwin Paul Rudolph, *The Martin Luther Treasury,* Wheaton, Illinois, Victor Books), 1979, p. 11.
2 James M. Houston, *I Believe in the Creator,* (Grand Rapids, Michigan, William B, Eerdmans Publishing Company, 1980), p. 15.

own personal credo or vision statement. When I first began writing I wrote out my own vision statement which said in effect that I was committed to the Christian philosophy of life in which beauty, goodness, truth, holiness, and love have their source in a personal relationship of the human self with God as He became manifest in Jesus Christ. I also concluded that since I had limited emotional energy to invest, I wanted to write about people whose life accomplishments and character piqued my interest.

On one occasion when asked to consider writing a biography of a person whom I felt was not compatible with most of my core values, I politely declined. Knowing beforehand who I was, and who I was not, I knew I could not sustain my emotional energy or personal involvement with a person whose story and personality I did not admire.

I. Finding Your Own Voice

Besides understanding the nature of your core values, it is important to find your own voice. Knowing you are not Hemingway, Faulkner, Kipling, or whoever your favorite author is, frees you to develop your unique writing style. It is perfectly acceptable to be aware of a particular writing style you admire even to the point that you may want to imitate, say Hemingway's lean, short sentence style, as long as you don't try to copy it. It's wise to always remember Yogi Berra's insightful philosophy, *If you can't imitate him, don't copy him.* It is important, therefore, to get in touch with your own emotions and feelings. Doing so will enable you to develop a voice that will be unique and distinctive from all others.

J. The Messenger is the Message

Most of us remember a revered teacher, pastor, priest or parent who when they told a story to illustrate a point, we believed them as much for their integrity as for the truth of the story they told. Dr. James Houston of Regent College, once told me, "It is as important from whom you hear the message as the message itself." Mark Noll writing in his book, *Turning Points, Decisive Moments in the History of Christianity,* makes this same point when he writes that early mission effectiveness usually, *Depended as much upon the [missioner's] plain virtue as upon more highly visible exertions in preaching and teaching.*[1]

K. Simon Birch

In the movie Simon Birch (based on the Novel, *Say a Prayer for Owen Meany* by John Irving), the storyteller declares it was through Simon Birch that he came to faith in God. Simon believed he was the Lord's mouthpiece. As the story unfolds, we discover this to be true. But like many creative people who have the strength of character to share themselves and be who they are, Simon was rejected by some of the very people who should have celebrated his uniqueness, including his parents and the minister of his church. Like Gutenberg, Martin Luther and others, Simon paid a price for his creativity. But Simon didn't care; he spoke and acted from the uniqueness of who he was.

L. The Quest

In literature, the metaphor for self-discovery is the quest or the journey. In mythology it is usually the king's youngest and least likely son to succeed to the throne. Nevertheless the son is given an assignment to bring back the Holy Grail or to slay the dragon deep in the forest. The journey is replete with great physical and moral challenges. Yet as the son overcomes each obstacle, he gains both physical and moral strength as he journeys from ignorance to understanding, from despair to rock-solid faith and an appreciation for what he had at home.

Readers of the New Testament will find a similarity in the story of the Prodigal Son. Returning home after a long absence helps one understand and celebrate the reality that each of us is the totality of our past influences. This includes our failures, accomplishments and friendships as well as our religious and racial backgrounds. This, as well as our personal religious faith, makes up our unique character and identity. This self-knowledge allows us to move into our profession as writers with humility, and with Paul's words from Galatians 6:3-4 as paraphrased in The Message by Eugene Peterson:

---

1   *Ibid.* p. 100.

Make a careful exploration of who you are and the work you have been given, and then sink yourself into that. Don't be impressed with yourself. Don't compare yourself with others. Each of you must take responsibility for doing the creative best you can for your own life. Galatians 6:3-4

M. Exercise

This exercise is designed to probe your own uniqueness. Write nine responses to the question, "Who am I?" and do the same for "Who am I not."

Chapter Four
The Creative Attitude, Part III.
Active Looking

You have seen things, but have paid no attention; your ears are open, but you hear nothing (Isaiah 42:20, NIV).

A Active Looking and Seeing

1. Thinking is not automatic

When Yogi Berra said, *It's amazing what you can see just by looking around,* he was telling us that seeing, listening and thinking are not automatic. My wife and I once lived and worked among the Otomi people in the Mezquital Valley of central Mexico. When I first saw the Mezquital Valley I was so caught up by my previous geographical conditioning and sense of place I did not, or would not allow room in my affections for a new reality. I was in love with the dense, green cedar and Douglas fir forests that run down to deep cool inlets and rocky seashores that I grew up with in the Pacific Northwest. The smell of cedar shingles, fir trees in the warm sun and the sight of the sun glinting off multicolored spinnakers and a diamond studded ocean filled with sailboats swelled my heart like music of a great symphony. At first glance there appeared to be nothing in the Mezquital that I could identify with. No trees, flowers or shrubs of the kind I knew, just an arid valley of scrub mesquite, maguey and cactus. I saw it as a place completely devoid of beauty. But over time, as I developed an appreciation for the landscape, I began to notice a new and different kind of beauty. Nowhere have I seen purple mountains like those of the Mezquital Valley in late afternoon. The play of dappled light on ever-moving fibrous clouds can change in a moment to dark nimbostratus clouds that block out the sun and give a mythical quality to the landscape of sparse plant life and bare soil. The gigantic panorama of alternating light and shadow across the valley floor is not unlike one might experience viewing the aurora borealis, only without the sharp dancing colors.

Upon reflection I have concluded that without knowing it people often become prisoners in a world of habit. In reality this is a constricted sense of self. Such an attitude can dull our perception and ability to see the loveliness of life, the uniqueness of people or place and thus hinder us from expanding our horizons. Leonardo da Vinci was reported to have said the key to awakening and enriching life's experiences was to awaken and refine one's sensory awareness.

B. Creative Attitude Takes Work

At the same time I admit that cultivating a creative attitude toward life doesn't happen automatically. Rather, it requires disciplining ones self to stay alert to everything that is happening around you. And more important, to stay alert to the things you see every day but hardly notice, like the color of a leaf in fall, and the curious question of a small child. Natural history writer, Barry Lopez illustrates what the act of disciplined looking and observing can do for one's prose:

> I watched dusk descend over the countryside. A nearly full moon rises yellow-orange in a deep blue-sky. Stout-legged horses graze in fields along the main road and herds of Holstein cattle drift toward the milking barns before sharp-voiced dogs.[1]

---

1   Barry Lopez, *About This Life: Journeys on the Threshold of Memory* (New York, Vintage Books, 1988) p. 46.

Lopez does not give the reader a litany of facts about what he sees. Rather, with specific concrete details he shows us the event that is before him. His details reveal his keen observation, his alive presence to the moment and his sensitive rapport with the landscape.

C. Looking for Details

Developing a creative attitude means actively looking for details that might escape you at first glance. It means looking with the eye of your mind to go beyond the surface of things to make mental connections with your surroundings. When I do research for a book or article, I actually ask myself the question, "What is it that I am seeing? What is here for me to discover that I did not see at first glance? And, what is happening to me that's important for the reader to know and understand?

1. Robert MacNeil

Once having isolated and become aware of the details surrounding a certain event, the writer (biographer) chooses words and images that convey how he or she felt about that event or memory. An example of this is a short story from Wordstruck (a memoir) by Robert MacNeil:

> It is a winter's night in 1936 in Halifax, Nova Scotia. A small boy is being read to. He is warm from a hot bath, wearing striped, flannel pajamas and a thick woolen dressing gown with a tasseled cord. He has dropped off his slippers to slide his bare feet between the cushions of the sofa.
>
> Outside, a salty wind blows snow against the panes of the windows. Foghorns are grumping far in the distance. The coal fire in the basket grate burns intense and silent. His mother reads:
>
> Whenever the moon and stars are set,

Whenever the wind is high,
All night long in the dark and wet,
A man goes riding by.

Late at night when the fires are out,

Why does he gallop and gallop about?

MacNeil said as a boy *Windy Nights* by Robert Louis Stevenson gave him a scary, yet exciting, feeling that outside in the dark there were things to be feared—but adventure too. It was, continued MacNeil:

> My first experience of being drawn into the spell cast by a story-teller was the discovery that words make another place, a place to escape with your spirit.[1]

Notice MacNeil's keen observation and listening skills. Outside, a salty wind blows against the windowpanes. Foghorns grump in the distance. A coal fire burns. Where and how? In a specific type of grate, and with a heat that is both intense and silent.

D. Being Alert to One's Senses

The importance of a writer looking and listening fully at the texture, shape, color, smells and sounds around him or her cannot be overstated. It is by being alert to one's senses that the writer is able to comprehend the full value of his or her physical world. And by understanding how these sounds, sights and smells relate to your subject, the writer can, by using imagery (figures of speech) and concrete details, stimulate the reader's own sense of sight, sound, taste, smell and touch. Attention to such details allows the writer to develop the subtleties and poetry of language. A rule of thumb for one writer was that on every page he wanted there to be at least two sensory details observed through the viewpoint character.

1. Davita's Harp

Note this small passage from Chaim Potok's book *Davita's Harp*. The young girl Davita is at the seashore recovering after a mental break-down brought on by the shock of the death of her father in the Spanish Civil War and the deportation of her favorite uncle:

---

1   Robert MacNeil, *Wordstruck*, (New York, Viking Penguin, 1989), p. 12.

The weeks of August went by as if in a drawn-out languorous dream. Slowly my strength returned. The warm sun, the vast and vaulting silence, the patient ministering of my aunt—all was healing balm to me that month. And one afternoon I wandered off the porch by myself and went carefully across the grassy slope and down to the beach. I felt the sand on my feet, coarser than the sand at Sea Gate, and touched the water with my hands, cool and calm and smooth. As far out as I could see were water and sky and horizon. How warm and sweet and clean all this wondrous ocean.[1]

E. Conveying Emotion Through Details

There is a great deal to learn from these two examples about the art of using concrete specific details in one's writing. However, the one thing I want to focus on here is an idea that comes from André Fontaine and William A. Gavin Jr. in their book *The Art of Writing Nonfiction* where they say:

> The details you see and choose to write must not only be true, but significant. They must convey more in perception or emotion–more than they do in words.[2]

An article written by Lynn Darling for *Esquire* about Tom Brokaw illustrates the way specific details can convey the emotion of a place:

1. Tom Brokaw's World

> Yankton, South Dakota lies on a bluff overlooking the Missouri River, a low-slung town of pickup trucks parked diagonally on a broad empty street, a place where both the Sunday sermon and the Saturday night saloon can count on collecting a crowd. The former territorial capital of the Dakotas, Yankton was the last stop on the riverboat's run, a jumping-off point, and a town that understood the language of last chances. It was a place where

---

1   Chaim Potok, *Davita's Harp*, (New York, Fawcett Columbine, 1985), p. 244.
2   André Fontaine and Williams A. Glavine, Jr., *The Art of Nonfiction Writing*, (New York, Syracuse University Press, 1987), p. 59.

outlaw Jack McCall was hanged for shooting Wild Bill Hickok, but that was as hot as it ever got here in Tom Brokaw's hometown.

In just over a hundred words, Darling has taken the reader into Brokaw's hometown, to let them see and feel what it is like to be there. We see this "low-slung town of pickups parked diagonally on a broad empty street" where both the Sunday morning sermon and the Saturday night saloon draw crowds, and presumably nothing else does for the rest of the week.[1]

F. How to Incorporate Sensory Images into One's Prose

Canadian photographer, Freeman Patterson, in his book, *Photography and the Art of Seeing*, helps us understand how we can be more aware of our physical world and incorporate these sensory images into our prose:

> When we look at a lake we are first aware of what the lake expresses. We see its tranquility or its turbulence, not its shape or color. When we see a face, the first thing we notice is what the face reveals—hostility, joy, sadness. The message is expressed by the sum of all the facial features. Our observation of each detail of the face comes later.[2]

G. Sense Memory

Have you ever wondered how it is that actors are able to weep or cry on cue? The answer: they have developed what the acting profession calls sense memory. If an actor has a scene that requires a display of deep emotion, the actor knows that emotion cannot be manufactured out of nothing. Thus, before going on stage, the actor will concentrate strongly on a personal incident in his or her life that had a profound personal emotional shock. It is through such realism that the depth of emotion is obtained. It is true also for the writer as well as the actor. Constantine

1 *Ibid.* p. 159.
2 Freeman Patterson, *Photography and the Art of Seeing*, (Toronto: Van Nostrand Reinhold, Ltd., 1979), p. 66.

Stanislavski in his book on *The Art of Acting* stressed that actors should forego external acting tricks to generate emotion. Rather he wanted actors to draw on reservoirs of their own experiences.

H. Drawing on Reservoirs of Your Own Experience

Let me underscore the words *drawing on reservoirs of your own experience.* Let's assume you are a skier and on one occasion you had the supreme experience of skiing down a mountain with the sun at your back through ten inches of fresh powder on newly waxed skis. Years later when you recalled that moment you will almost be able to feel the cool bite of the air around your face hear the sound of highly polished skis swishing through the snow. You will relive the exhilarating sense of joy, freedom and happy abandonment as you soared over a ledge and flew as if you could fly forever.

When you transfer your feelings about the joy of skiing into your narrative, your readers (if they are skiers or want to be) will say (perhaps not consciously), "Aha! these are not just empty words. I know what that feeling is like." At this point you have built identification and the reader will believe you because they have experienced similar emotions and feelings.

I. I Saw Gooley Fly

In a wonderful older book called *I Saw Gooley Fly*, author Joe Bayly tells the strange tale of a college freshman named Gooley who one day steps out of his third-story dorm window and to the surprise of his dorm mates, doesn't fall to the ground. He simply flies off into the wild blue yonder. Have you ever felt so joyous about something that happened to you that you said, "It felt like I was walking on air?" Joe Bayly took those subjective, metaphysical feelings and applied them to an individual who had undergone a born-again spiritual conversion and personifies them in a story/parable about an unlikely university freshman named Gooley.

The story is humorous, but not trivial. The feelings that accompany faith and growth in God's love are profoundly important and meaningful to an individual believer. Because people are not robots, they have a capacity to experience the full range of human emotion: love, wonder, jealousy, confusion, fear, stress, happiness, and more. Bayly wrote his book during a time when some in the church thought feelings were suspect. Bayly's story explores the reality that feelings about one's faith are as important and meaningful as are the historical facts of one's faith. Those who recall what it was like to be forgiven and released from a burden of guilt by reason of their personal faith in Jesus Christ can identify with Gooley's ecstatic joy and sudden urge to want to fly. So, too, does the person who experiences the rapturous joy of first love.

1. , Painful Feelings

On the other hand, it goes without saying that not all memories are pleasurable. In fact most people seem to remember more unhappy moments than pleasurable ones. For the writer, this is where the deep wells of creativity often reside. It has been said that the best writing comes out of pain, yours or someone else's. The reason seems to be that the most valuable and most potent insights into our humanity occur during moments of crisis, self-doubt, frustration, uncertainty, fear, and indeed pain.

One memory that can cause me deep emotional pain has to do with the near-death experience of my beautiful 28-year-old daughter. It happened in October. And each October, if I allow my memory to recall that event I can suddenly have a dry mouth, my stomach will feel hollow and the full pain and the memory returns with a jolt just by employing my sense memory.

I once saw a man struck down in Mexico City. After forty years, I can, in my mind still hear the bang of that yellow cab striking him. I can see the man's face, laughing and looking the wrong way as he crossed the street. The squeal of the brakes is in my ears yet. I can still see the mud falling from underneath the left fender as he was struck.

I can also recall the painful night my wife learned her mother had a stroke. Even as I write this I can see my wife standing in the middle of the room crying and speaking into the telephone, "I love you, Mom. You are the best mother anyone ever had. I love you, I love you." Out across the miles I can still hear that plaintive cry, "I love you, I love you, I love you, Mom." I wept then, and I weep again remembering.

J. Getting in Touch With One's Feelings

What does all this mean for the writer? It means simply the writer must know how to empathize with a subject's intense feelings. When your subject expresses feelings of being vulnerable or out of control, or in pain over the loss of a loved one, the biographer should have in his or her memory bank or in a file, diary or journal, expressions and feelings of how they or others felt under similar circumstances.

Every human at one time in his or her life has felt an absence of love. Most of us have had feelings of longing, grief, being in distress, of yearnings and sadness of envy, jealousy, of guilt, anger and wanting a wrong to be made right. Knowing how to honestly identify and empathize with these and other feelings and emotions are what it means to be an empathetic person and a sensitive writer. When writers use emotions and feeling in their writing their hope is that the reader also will experience the same emotions in the same way as the character did. If you are a writer of children's literature, remembering what it felt like when you were in the third grade and a friend didn't want to sit beside you on the school bus could mean the difference between success and failure of your story.

1. J. K. Rowlings

The success of the Harry Potter books by author J. (Joanne) K. Rowlings range from the wonderful use of nonsense words for places and characters, like the strange boarding school called *Hogwarts* where students spend their time without adult supervision, to the hero's ability to move about on a flying broomstick. While the stories appeal to both children and adults, the hunger for enchantment (as did C.S. Lewis's Narnian Chronicles and Tolkien's Hobbit and Lord of the Ring stories) is, I believe, the principal reason for the success of Rowlings' books. Her gift is the ability to feel like an eleven-year-old child and express those feelings in her prose. Referring to the cover story in *Time* that featured the magic of *Harry Potter*, Rowlings said, "I can with no difficulty think myself back to eleven years old, (Harry's age.)."

2. Are Some Emotions More Correct Than Others?

There are those who believe that some emotions are more correct than others. Some religious groups believe a "spiritual" Christian is one who is always optimistic, contented, successful, warm and open, never expresses anger, and never becomes depressed, forlorn or disquieted in any way. They believe such a person is always in attendance at Sunday worship and all midweek programs and meetings. If a believer should fail in these areas they are often considered to be sub-Christian and in some quarters, sinful. Notice I put the word spiritual in quotation marks. Notwithstanding the large number of books that were written in the nineties on spirituality and spiritual direction, these terms have come under scrutiny by some who say:

> The term *spirituality* has at times been used so loosely that one researcher has called it a "fuzzy" concept that "embraces obscurity with passion."

3. Thomas Merton

My answer to this issue of "fuzzy" spirituality comes from Thomas Merton's, *Thoughts in Solitude*:

> It would be absurd to suppose that because emotion sometimes interferes with reason it therefore has no place in the spiritual life. Christianity is not stoicism. The cross does not sanctify us by destroying human feelings. Detachment is not insensibility. Too many ascetics fail to become great saints precisely because their rules and ascetic practices have merely deadened their humanity instead of setting it free to develop richly, in all its capacities, under the influence of grace. If we are without human feelings we cannot love God in the way in which we are meant to love Him—as men [and women]. If we do not respond to human affection we cannot be loved by God in the way Jesus has willed to love us—with the heart of the man, Jesus, who is God, the Son of God, the anointed Christ.

K. Not By Bread Alone

The following, by an unknown author, says what I want to say more profoundly than I ever could about rediscovering the beauty and loveliness of common ordinary everyday things around us. More importantly it pulls back the curtain to reveal what I believe is the essence of what it means to have a creative attitude. It's called *Not by Bread Alone*:

> Not by bread alone, but by the splendor of the firmament at night, the glory of the heavens at dawn, the blending of colors at sunrise, the loveliness of magnolia trees, the magnificence of mountains.

> Not by bread alone, but by the majesty of ocean breakers, the shimmer of moonlight on a calm lake, the flashing silver of a mountain torrent, the exquisite patterns of snow crystals, the creation of artists.

> Not by bread alone, but by the sweet song of a mocking bird, the rustle of wind in the trees, the magic of a violin, the sublimity of a softly lighted cathedral.

> Not by bread alone, but by the fragrance of roses, the scent of orange blossoms, the smell of new-mown hay, the clasp of a friend's hand, the tenderness of a mother's kiss.

> Not by bread alone, but by the lyrics of poets, the wisdom of sages, the holiness of saints, the biographies of great souls.

> Not by bread alone, but by comradeship and high adventure, seeking and finding, serving and sharing, loving and being loved. Man [and woman too] does not live by bread alone, but by being faithful in prayer, responding to the guidance of the Holy Spirit, finding and doing the will of God, now and eternally.

Chapter Five

Biography, Part I

The first law of history is not to lie; the second is not to be afraid to tell the truth. Leo XIII

A. What is Biography?

John Dryden (1631-1700), an English writer and poet laureate, seems to be the first person to define biography, as *The History of Particular Men's Lives.* (Note he did not include women, which tells us something about English culture and attitudes toward women in the last half of the seventeenth century!) The idea of biography, however, goes back to ancient times, to Beowulf and the exploits of early Anglo-Saxon legendary warriors. The purpose was to glorify or commemorate a person's greatness and to promote morality and high virtue of early saints. Writers of these early stories of saints, kings and other English historical figures conveniently overlooked their subjects' faults and shortcomings. They painted a picture of characters, settings and events nonexistent in the real world. Such over-praise, glorification and idealization of the saints and kings produced a literature that came to be known as *hagiography.* To this day, some biographies of notable people still suffer from an overblown worshipful treatment of the subject. Fortunately, *A Handbook To*

Literature gives the biographer a more realistic understanding of what biography should be:

> Today, biography may be defined as the accurate presentation of the life history from birth to death of an individual, this presentation being secured through an honest effort to interpret the facts of the life in such a way so as to offer a unified impression of the character, mind and personality of the subject.[1]

In his book, *The End of History and the Last Man,* Francis Fukuyama tells us the first truly universal histories in the Western tradition were Christian:

> While there were Greek and Roman efforts to write histories of the known world, it was Christianity that first introduced the concept of equality of all men [and women] in the sight of God, and thereby conceived of a shared destiny for all peoples of the world. A Christian such as Saint Augustine had no interest in the particular history of the Greeks or Jews as such; what mattered was the redemption of man as man, an event that would constitute the working out of God's plan for mankind. Christianity, moreover, introduced the concept of a history that was finite in time, beginning with God's creation of man and ending with his final salvation. For Christians, the Day of Judgment that would usher in the kingdom of heaven would mark the end of earthly history.[2]

I therefore consider the writing of biography and history to be Kingdom work and a vital part of God's plan for mankind. Historian Milan Hubl said, *The first step in liquidating a people is to erase its memory.* And I would also add *language.* Theologians and sociologist both affirm that shared rituals and the language we use form our realities. The insidious practice of slave owners to separate slaves from their language families

---

1 C. Hugh Holman, *A Handbook to Literature* (Indianapolis: Bobbs-Merrill Education Publishing, 1980) pp.25,26.

2 Francis Fukuyama, *The End of History,* and *The Last Man* (New York, Maxwell Macmillan, Inc. 1992), p.56.

was a cultural and moral evil as tyrannical as the act of slavery itself. One's common language, after all, is the glue that holds together one's collective history. The tyranny of slavery not only deprived individuals of their personal liberty, by also robbed them of their inner sense of self. Thus stories, histories, sagas, traditions and biographies of all kinds help us all to be infused with courage and a greater self-confidence and inner reality about who we are and what we can become.

B. The Biographer's Role

The Greek word *history* which is what a biography is, simply means to inquire in order to tell how it was. This, I contend is exactly the role of the biographer, i.e., to bring to light or to make visible what, without you, might perhaps have never been seen. Whether we realize it or not, people wear disguises. A man can hide behind a beard or a particular tone of voice or even the clothes he wears. While clothes protect us from the elements, they also protect us from psychological exposure. Knowing that people wear disguises, the biographer's task is to get beyond the disguise to reveal the essence of the individual. In addition to wearing disguises, people are full of complex contradictions and mixed motives. J. P. Morgan is reputed to have once said: "There are two reasons why a man does anything. There's the good reason, and there is the real reason." To which William Zinsser in his useful book *Extraordinary Lives* adds: "The modern biographer's task is to find the real reason."[1]

C. Six Classes or Kinds of Biography

Not all biographies are exactly the same. I personally identify six different classes of biography:

(1) Biography (standard or classic)
(2) Autobiography
(3) Life and Times Biography.
(4) Memoir Biography.
(5) Profile Biography
(6) Historical Novel

---

1   Peter P. Jacobi, *Writing the Personality Profile* (*The Writer's Year Book*, 1990), p. 24.

D. Historical or Classic Biography

The historical biography attempts to interpret the important aspects of an individual's life and career from birth until death. This means showing a person's individual characteristics, career accomplishments, personality, habits, motives and the impact for good or ill the subject made on society. Some biographers display a subject's many accomplishments, but do not reveal their ambiguities, misjudgments or shortcomings.

1. Doris Kearns Goodwin

Doris Kearns Goodwin received a Pulitzer Prize for her monumental book on the life of Franklin and Eleanor Roosevelt during World War II. Clearly FDR was a transformational President. The shape of America and indeed the world might well have been tragically different if it hadn't been for FDR's insight, vision, humor, optimism and moral courage during the early years of World War II. Yet juxtaposed with his great strengths, Goodwin allows us to see FDR's misjudgments, ego, blind spots and his moral weakness, thus creating a fully developed three-dimensional human being, rather than a one-dimensional cardboard caricature.

2. Biographical Sources

Information for the historical biography comes from written archival documents, personal letters, diaries, journals, plus autobiographies as well as from personal interviews of family, friends, colleagues and even enemies who knew the individual. Interviewing a person's enemy can sometimes ensure greater objectivity and offset the bias of others who might be less objective in their opinion of the subject.

3. Authorized and Unauthorized Biography

I should also make the distinction between authorized and unauthorized biography. An authorized biography simply means the subject or the family cooperates by allowing the biographer access to the subject's private papers. This was true for me when I wrote about Wycliffe founder William Cameron Townsend. I was given complete access to and freedom to use the Townsend Archives. An unauthorized biographer usually has to hunt and struggle on his or her own without the subject's cooperation or that of the subject's family and friends.

E. Autobiography

Thomas Cahill in his book *How the Irish Saved Civilization* tells us that it was the early Church father Augustine [354-430] who was the first human being to say "I" and mean what we mean today. Cahill concludes therefore, that Augustine's confessions is the first genuine autobiography in human history: Augustine tells us everything, his jealousies in infancy, his thieving as a boy, his stormy relationship with his overbearing mother (the ever-certain Monica), his years of philandering, his breakdowns and his shameful love for an unnamed peasant woman.[1]

When I read an autobiography of a notable person for research purposes I usually expect it to be, as one person said, "Either half-truths or one-and one-half truths." For obvious reasons, self-disclosure is painful. Most people are selective about the material they want to share with the public. Mark Twain once said to Rudyard Kipling:

> An autobiography is the only one work in which a man against his own will and in spite of his utmost striving to the contrary, reveals himself in his true light to the world.

> However, in a genuine autobiography, I believe it is impossible for a man to tell the truth about himself or to avoid impressing the reader with the truth about himself.[2]

At the same time serious readers of American literature understand, that autobiography and memoir (which is closely related to biography) have dominated American culture throughout the last half of the twentieth century).

There are number of helpful books devoted exclusively to helping a person write his or her own story. *Legacy* by Linda Spence, published by Swallow Press guides the writer through the various stages of life

1 Thomas Cahill, How *The Irish Saved Civilization*, (New York: Nan A. Talese/Doubleday 1995), pp. 39, 41.
2 Rudyard Kipling, A *Kipling Pageant*, (New York, Garden City, Doubleday, Doran & Company, Inc. 1935), p. 405.

from childhood, adolescence, marriage, parenthood, middle adult years and finally, being a grandparent.   Each section has a series of thought-provoking-questions designed to trigger one's memory bank. Example: *Who were your friends and what did you do together?*

F. Life and Times Biography

Life and times biography is exactly what the name says. The biographer is concerned with two principal subjects: the central figure of the story and the time or era in which the subject lived. While the writer covers the items required for an historical biography, a life-and-times biography centers more attention on a certain historical period or a significant or pivotal part of an individual's life. In addition to helping the reader understand the character and motivation of the subject (this is common to all biography), life and times biography is concerned with helping the reader understand what it was like for your subject to have lived during a specific period in history. A life and times biography will explore the prevailing ideas, philosophies, social and political pressures of the time.

For example, as late as 1903, U.S. president Grover Cleveland said, "Sensible and responsible women do not want the vote." In 1943, IBM president Thomas J. Watson said: "I think there is a world market for about five computers." In the popular imagination, computers were fearful Huxleyan mechanical brains and robot machines. A memoir published in 1999 about the opening up of the KGB files reveals that Ethel and Julius Rosenberg, who were convicted in 1957 of espionage for the Soviet Union and later executed, would have been spared the death sentence in the nineties. A life and times biography of the Rosenbergs written in the nineties would have helped the reader in the twenty-first century understand the mood of the American people and the feelings they had against what was generally believed to be a serious threat to America's national security in the fifties. We now know this was mostly paranoia and a terrible constriction of social ideas.

G. Memoir Biography

The principal difference between a memoir and other classes of biography is that the memoir writer personally knew, and had some kind of relationship with the subject. This allows the writer to include personal recollections and anecdotes about the subject. Admittedly the distinctions between these various kinds of biography sometimes overlap. However, memoir biography is unique. Memoir gives the writer more latitude to paraphrase or to give his or her impressions or the gist of events. The requirements for the memoir biographer remain the same as for all classes of biography, namely; to gather the facts of a person's life and to digest, organize and interpret them. Then using story telling techniques, weave a narrative with a beginning, middle and ending. The end result of biography of whatever kind you write should have developed a character sufficiently to give the reader a new perspective and psychological understanding of your subject.

1. Memoir Biography is Often Selective

While sharing the same general style and purpose of classic biography, memoir biography may sometimes have to be read with a certain reserve, particularly if a person is writing one's own memoir. Letters that appear in memoir, or from which source material is reported to have come, may or may not have been spontaneous. Such letters and other information could be highly selective or colored by various prejudices and self-interest.

2. Frank McCourt—*Angela's Ashes*

Frank McCourt insists his book; *Angela's Ashes* is a memoir and not an autobiography. Nor does not want to be locked into writing a factual reconstruction of events. His intention is to give a gist or impression of what happened. At the same time, it is important to understand that *Angela's Ashes* is no less true because McCourt doesn't give a word-for-word documented account of his conversations.

3. Travel Memoirs and Bernal Diaz del Castillo

Most everyone has kept a diary or journal of his or her travels or vacation trips. Afterward such journals are often put on a shelf never to be read. Happily for posterity, many of the early explorers and adventurers developed travel journaling to a fine art. In some cases these early first-person accounts are the only historic record we have of an ex-traordinary moment in time.

Perhaps one of the most famous historical memoirs is *The Discovery and Conquest of Mexico* by Bernal Diaz del Castillo (the original title was *The True History of the Conquest of New Spain*). Bernal Diaz describes himself as an eyewitness to the conquest under Cortez. From him we have for all time that marvelous description of what Mexico City looked like in 1440-1450:

> When we saw so many cites and villages in the waters of the lake and other towns on dry land, and the straight, level cause-way leading into Mexico City, we were amazed and we said that it was like the enchanted things related in the book of Amadis because of the huge towers, temples, and masonry buildings ris-ing from the water. Some of the soldiers even asked whether the things we saw were not a dream.[1]

4. Theodore Roosevelt

Theodore Roosevelt's book, *Through the Brazilian Wilderness*, pub-lished in 1914, gives us a view of Roosevelt's feelings and state of mind as he beholds what no white person had seen before, the giant River of Doubt that was later renamed the Roosevelt River in his honor:

> The river now widened, so that in places, it looked like a long lake; it wound in every direction through the endless marshy plain, whose surface was broken here and there by low moun-tains. The splendor of the sunset I never saw surpassed. We were steaming east toward clouds of storm. The river ran, a broad highway of molten gold, into the flaming sky; the far-off mountains loomed purple across the marshes; belts of rich green, the river banks stood out on either side against the rose hues of the rippling water; in front, as we forged steadily on-ward, hung the tropic night, dim and vast.[2]

---

1   Bernal Diaz del Castillo, *The Discovery and Conquest of Mexico*, (New York: Grove Press, Inc. 1956), p. XV.
2   Theodore Roosevelt, *Through the Brazilian Wilderness*,

The following is an example of a more recent travel memoir writing that is hard, sharp and specifically concrete and employs vivid word pictures:

> In the summer of 1989, two years before the Gulf War, I traveled to Iraq to see the ruins of Babylon and the Tower of Babel. It was a journey I had long wanted to make. Reconstructed between 1899 and 1917 by the German archaeologist Robert Koldewey. Babylon lies about forty miles south of Baghdad—a huge maze of butter-colored walls that once was the most powerful city on earth, close to a clay mound which the guidebooks say is all that is left of a tower God cursed with multiculturalism.[1]

H. Profile Biography research will be concise. While the research for a profile may not be as exhaustive as with a full-blown biography, the profile biographer must nevertheless spend time—often a considerable amount of time-observing the subject and interviewing friends and colleagues.

Note I used the plural friends and colleagues. Too many profiles are written only after a single interview. (I have been guilty of doing this more than once). Often this means the writer hasn't taken the time to interview people who knew the subject when they were younger and less well known. Nor has the writer spent time observing the subject either at home, or interacting with friends, children or colleagues. And in many cases, the profile writer has neglected to gather insights and information from a spouse.

Remember too, your profile will be more colorful and have greater human interest if you use the same literary devices of narrative hook (see anecdotal lead), character development, description, point of view, sense of place and forward action that leads to a satisfactory conclusion.

I. The Historical Novel

---

1   Alberto Manguel, *A History of Reading*, (New York, Penguin Books, 1996), p. 177.

Strictly speaking, the historical novel is not in the same category as a classical biography. However, I include it here as a sub-class of biography because the historical novel is often the most revealing of human nature. People in the former Soviet Union read historical novels as a way to understand their own social history. Novels usually examine human identity and individuality, which, in turn, reveals great truths about faith, temptation, loyalties, greed, godliness, and the whole spectrum of what it means to be human. Perhaps the single best example of this is Leo Tolstoy's Anna Karenina.

J. Where to Begin? (The Anecdotal Lead)

Throughout this book I have talked about the biographer as one who tells a story rather than simply imparting information. In order to make one's story as entertaining and informative as possible the biographer must be aware of the fundamental reality that the reader is a listener whose attention must be held. I have referred to this as trying to make the reader as comfortable as possible.

One of the most satisfying narrative comforts is for a story to have a coherent whole, with a beginning, middle and ending. Usually, however, you don't begin your narrative at the very beginning of your subject's life. The most compelling way to begin a story is with a dramatic anecdotal lead (often called the narrative hook) that pulls the reader into the story with the promise of more to follow. The anecdote is an interesting or dramatic short account of an event, an incident, a startling statement description or a summary lead that can usually stand alone. I once began a story by using the startling statement lead:

> Rain doesn't fall in the south-central state of Puebla, Mexico, it is thrown. Ten feet per year. Mules and men slip, slide and sink to their knees in oozy red mud. Sunlight seldom penetrates the overhanging trees along the main trade route leading from the Sierra Aztec village of Tatoscac to the Gulf of Mexico.[1]

1. Two Rules of Thumb

---

1   Hugh Steven and James C. Hefley, *Miracles in Mexico*, (Chicago, Moody Press, 1972), p. 51.

While the choice of beginnings is arbitrary, I personally employ two rules of thumb. One is that I try to select an anecdote that best illustrates the beginning of what the story is about. This could be an incident that occurred midway in the subject's life or career. If you begin with an anecdote that occurs midway or even late in the subject's life you can then flash back to an earlier time and then trace the events as they unfold in your subject's life.

My second rule of thumb for beginnings is that I like to begin a story the way I would pick up a puppy. You don't pick up a puppy by the head or by the tail. You pick it up somewhere behind the front paws. Always keeping in mind that you build your story by selecting incidents, stories and words that move the action forward. The classic procedure for story construction is "rising action," "climax" and "falling action" or denouement.

2. Cry The Beloved Country

I believe one of the most beautiful and descriptive leads in English literature is from Alan Paton's book *Cry the Beloved Country:*

> There is a lovely road that runs from Ixopo into the hills. These are grass-covered and rolling, and are lovely beyond any singing of it. The road climbs seven miles into them, to Carisbrook; from there, if there is no mist, you look down on one of the fairest valleys of Africa. About you there is grass and bracken and you may hear the forlorn crying of the tithoya, one of the birds of the veldt.[1]

One of my most favorite leads is Arthur Gordon's interview with an immortal from his book *A Touch of Wonder.* Cleverly, Gordon keeps the reader in suspense for almost two pages before we learn who the person is he has come to visit:

> The month was June; the English weather was blue and gold. The world was young, and so was I. But driving down from Oxford in the old Sunbeam I had borrowed for the occasion, I felt my assurance deserting me.

1 Alan Paton, *Cry, The Beloved Country,* (New York, Charles Scribners and Sons, 1959), p. 3.

The great man was almost a recluse now, and it was said that he did not care for Americans...When I found the somber seventeenth-century house and saw my host walking down to the gate to meet me, I grew so flustered that I hardly knew whether to shake his hand or turn and run.

He was so small! The crown of his floppy hat that he wore was not much higher than my shoulder, and I doubt if he weighed 120 pounds. His skin was dark for an Englishman; his mustache was almost white. His eyebrows were as thick and tangled as marsh grass, but behind the gold-rimmed glasses his eyes were bright as a terrier's. He was sixty-nine years old.

He saw instantly how ill at ease I was. "Come in, come in," he said...He led me still speechless to a pond at the end of his garden where there was his so-called navy: a six-foot skiff with a hand-cranked paddle wheel. "You can be the engine room," he said. "I'll be the passenger list." I was so agitated that I cranked too hard. The paddle wheel broke and there I was marooned in the middle of a fishpond with Rudyard Kipling. He began to laugh and so did I, and the ice was broken.[1]

E. Who, What, Where, When, How and Why

I hope you noticed in these examples of beginnings the use of specific details, and how quickly the reader knew who the actors were, what was happening, where they were geographically, when the action was happening and how and why the action was taking place. This is a calculated literary device known simply as, who, what, where, when, how and why. Some modern writers think this literary device is no longer in fashion. But I believe you will have a better book or article if you let the reader know, what is happening, where it is happening, and to whom it is happening-all in the first couple of paragraphs. This not only hooks your reader, it establishes the underlying theme or central idea of your story. There are some exceptions, of course, as in the case of Arthur Gordon's story of meeting Rudyard Kipling, the author of Jungle Book,

---

1   Arthur Gordon, *A Touch of Wonder*, (Old Tappan, New Jersey, Spire Books, 1983), p. 57.

Mowgli, and Gunga Din. In this case we were kept in suspense about the identity of Kipling until the sixth paragraph. Notice, however, that Gordon skillfully kept the tension and suspense high until the moment when Kipling and Gordon, and we the reader, all laughed together.

The interesting fact to notice in each of these examples is that the stories do not follow in chronological order. If you were to read the full story you would notice that the opening and order of the story are designed to keep the reader in suspense for as long as possible. Later the authors flash back to earlier scenes to fill in the background.

Once again the reason for adopting this methodology of story telling is that the biographer selects the events in a person's life that seem to be the most significant. Since many of the important anecdotes in an individual's life do not happen chronologically, the writer may end the story with an anecdote that sums up the subject's life.

K. Conclusion

Just as the beginning of your story is arbitrary, so too is the ending. But like beginnings that are difficult, endings can be more difficult still. I often include an epilogue or a "Word to the Reader" or an "Afterword" as a way of tying up loose ends and bringing a sense of closure to the story. One of the pitfalls for any writer to avoid is to end the story with a spelled-out moral. The whole story should be the moral. And at all costs the reader should not get the impression that the author has in some way created a contrivance to make the story have a "happy" ending.

In an earlier day, one of the famous Hollywood directors insisted his movies end with the hero, usually a child, crying as his best friend's dog or horse died or was being sent away. The director was captive to the old show-business maxim: "Always leave them laughing or crying."

It is not a contrivance, however, to end your story full circle. If it is not possible to do this at the conclusion of your story, then by all means use an epilogue or an afterword. These are basic literary devices that will give your reader that necessary sense of closure.

1. The Snapper

One literary device that many writers use to conclude their story is called the snapper. A snapper, like the opening lead of your story, is a pointed anecdote or quote that in some way summarizes the main theme of your story. If I do not have a satisfactory concluding "snapper," I will occasionally ask my subject or someone who had intimate knowledge of the subject to write a concluding afterword. This is the afterword that Don Webster wrote to conclude my book, *Good Broth to Warm Our Bones:*

> As I left Barrow [Alaska] and the plane took me back to my new world as Associate Pastor of Forward Baptist Church in Cambridge Ontario, my mind flew back to the dedication of the Inupiat New Testament. One of the first people to buy the New Testament was old Nrgovana, a man who had known hard times when people starved to death because they has missed the yearly Caribou migrations. With a smile as big as an Arctic sunburst, he held out his New Testament and said, "Now God's Word is in Eskimo, me no starve no more."[1]

This ending illustrated my own preference for how stories should end, namely, they should be positive, upbeat and express some sense of hope and expectation for the future. About leads and endings, Peter Jacobi said:

> One leads and ends not with the predictable but with the unusual, the inexplicable, the extraordinary, the comic, the dramatic, the poignant, and the memorable.[2]

Finally, when you have finished your story, stop writing. I once read a story about a man who was watching an artist paint a portrait. The portrait really was finished but the artist kept fussing around with a little dab here and a brush stroke there. Finally the artist threw down his brush in exasperation. "Every artist," he said, "should have someone standing behind him with a big wooden mallet to hit him smartly on the head when the painting is finished. Same goes for writers."

---

1   Hugh Steven, *Good Broth to Warm our Bones*, Crossway Books, (Westchester, Illinois, 1982), p 206
2   Ibid, p 27.

Chapter Six

Biography, Part II

A. What I Ask Myself Before I Write

"How do you choose your subjects?" is a question I am asked frequently. Early in my career I had two experiences that helped formulate my personal credo for the kind of people I wanted to write about.

1. How can you write about someone nobody likes?

When I first began writing, I was alive with creative energy and idealism. I willingly wrote about anyone and anything that was presented to me. Then one day a film producer asked me if I would consider writing a biography about a wealthy businessman. The film producer offered me ten thousand dollars up front to write the book. In the seventies, that was almost as much money as I made in a year. However, all things were not as they seemed. When I began to interview this man's friends and colleagues, I found them strangely noncommittal. I felt as if I were swimming through mud. Finally, one brave person summed it up for all the others when she said, "How can you write about someone nobody likes?" I didn't.

2. The Converted Witch

The second experience came when one of my publishers asked me to interview a witch who had been converted to Christianity. The man was in demand as a speaker partly because he drove around speaking in churches and schools in a van he called a Witchmobile.

3. Is This Someone I Want to Introduce to My Friends?

Within minutes after meeting the converted witch he began asking me how much money I thought he would make from the book. I suppose that is a legitimate question. Except when a person's first interest is money rather than the ministry to the Body, I am uneasy. Furthermore, unless your name is linked to some late-breaking news story or you are a high-profile celebrity, book publishing is not the way to make your fortune. However, the incident that tipped the scales against my involvement in the story came when I observed his condescending attitude toward his wife when she timidly asked for grocery money. From that observation and several other incidents, I decided I did not want to spend the next six months or more delving into this person's past. He, frankly, was not the kind of person I wanted to introduce to my friends.

B. Narratives of Grace

In his insightful book *How the Irish Saved Civilization*, Thomas Cahill speaks for me when he says:

> History is also the narratives of grace, the recounting of those blessed and inexplicable moments when someone did something for someone else, saved a life, bestowed a gift, gave something beyond what was required.[1]

These are some of the first things I look for in a subject when I consider writing a biography. In a word, I want to write about people whose life, accomplishments and personal character will in some way be an inspiration to others. I also resonate with Russian novelist Boris

1 Thomas Cahill, *How the Irish Saved Civilization* (New York, Doubleday Dell Publishing Group, Inc 1995), p VI.

Pasternak who said he wanted to write about something that was deep and true.

Biography requires enormous amounts of emotional, spiritual and physical energy, not to mention the time it takes to do research and writing. As a purely arbitrary and personal preference, I would, therefore, prefer to write about a person I can admire. Please note that in no way do I suggest my personal criteria to be binding or normative for any biographer. I admit an appreciation and a certain fascination for many important books on historical figures whose personal lives and the effect they had on history were less than exemplary. Since I have a concern for the historical record, and if given the opportunity, I could, in all probability, find it a challenge to examine the motives and life of a controversial historical figure.

C. Drama (Conflict, Suspense, Deliverance, Resolution)

Other criteria I look for are the basic elements or bare bones of story telling. Namely: conflict, suspense, crisis, deliverance and resolution. Or simply, is there enough inherent drama in the story to keep people turning the pages to find out what happens next. One of the best definitions of story is: It is a piece of writing that makes the reader want to find out what happens next.

The Greek word "drama" means action. A walk across the room is action, but in good drama, the reader shares the emotion of the character that, for whatever reason, walks across the room. When I look for drama, I don't mean mad car chases or bursting bombs. These are often the clichés of inane television action. Rather than stereotypes, I look for surprises in human behavior. Drama can come from the way a person uses language or their incongruities that can be translated into character scenes and situations.

1. Tidy Mind But No Poetry

Often the simple everyday events of life can reveal a person's character and provide interesting drama. Once on a business trip I stayed with a man whose daily routine never varied. He ate the same dried-cereal-and-toast breakfast every morning. Every morning he left for work at precisely the same time, stopped at the same newsstand, bought the same newspaper, and with barely a glance at the headlines, opened the paper to the financial page. At lunch he sat down to the same brown-bag lunch. After carefully saving his sandwich bag and wrapping, he returned to work and left precisely at quitting time to return home by the exact same route. I concluded that my host had a tidy mind, but lived life without much poetry. At the same time, his strict ordinariness provided a certain drama that one could use with great effect as an interesting character study. Like the man I once wrote about who used to crack a raw egg in his coffee and ate a head of lettuce like one might eat an apple, all wonderful idiosyncrasies!

D. Drama of the Ordinariness

1. James Herriot Stories

When I think of the drama of the ordinariness, the delightful James Herriot animal stories come to mind. In reality these stories are more about the idiosyncrasies of people interacting with their animals and environment than they are about animals themselves.

2. *Upstairs, Downstairs*

The successful TV series of maids, butlers, cooks and the people they served in *Upstairs, Downstairs* was also a wonderful example of the drama of the ordinary. And what of the ordinary everyday routine of an old fisherman, past his prime, struggling to keep his catch that became high drama in Ernest Hemingway's *The Old Man and the Sea?*

3. *This Tender Land*

One of the most satisfying and heartfelt dramatic moments I have known was in experiencing a little-known Aaron Copeland opera called *This Tender Land.* It's a simple story of a young farm girl on the eve of her high school graduation and the conflict she encounters between herself and her family, as she desires to leave the farm for a new life in the city. The opera is performed outdoors with the sky and open fields, dappled light, or in some cases rain as a backdrop. It may sound trite or outdated, but when the father stands on the porch of a real Midwest farmhouse and slowly sings, "Shall We Gather at the River," I am moved to quiet tears. The reason is I see myself in the story. I have felt the pain of an empty nest. I have experienced the nostalgia of home-coming, of family gatherings, of children who want their independence. This Tender Land is everyone's story that longs for family and has known the full range of common human emotions.

E. Emotion (Feelings)

Another criterion I look for has to do with emotion. In several other places throughout this book, in a variety of different ways, I have said I believe most people are propelled toward an action more by their emotions than by logical reasoning. Knowing this, the writer looks for and selects anecdotes, stories and events and places them in the narrative in a way that will touch the heartstrings of the reader. By emotional writing I am not talking about using emotional adjectives or sensualism. I am talking about writing the story as it happened with close attention (selection is an appropriate word) to those aspects of the story that will trigger an emotional response in my reader's heart and mind.

1. Charles Dickens

Someone asked Charles Dickens about his rules of composition and the artistic principles by which he proceeded. He said, I have only one artistic principle, that is, to rouse the emotions of my readers. "The heart has reasons which reason does not know," said the philosopher-saint, Blaise Pascal (Pensées 277). That is to say, human thought and action are influenced in a decisive manner by what happens to the heart. Edward Teller, principal architect of the hydrogen bomb, said he was "governed as much by feelings as by logic."

2. Manuel Arenas

In my book *Manuel*, there is an event that illustrates what I mean by allowing the inherent emotion in the story to come out all unbidden without too much overwriting from the author. The incident surrounds the young girl Luz, Manuel's mother, who has defied tribal tradition and protocol by refusing to marry the man her parents have selected for her. This refusal to marry Mariano, has caused great embarrassment and no small financial setback to Luz's father:

When the president came to the routine question, "Do you love Mariano?" Luz lifted her head and looked at the president. There was a long moment of silence. Then before Mariano and the parents knew what had happened, Luz screamed a defiant "No!" and raced out of the courthouse and up the hill to her hut to wait for the inevitable. Sooner than expected, her father bolted through the door and wrenched his woven tumpline off the wall. Without a word, he plunged it into a water jug and waited until the fibers became swollen and heavy.

Luz crouched in a corner, saying not a word, but pleading desperately with her eyes for her father not to strike her. With the first blow she knew her father's anger was uncontrollable. Blow after blow fell on her slender body, and they stopped only when her father became exhausted. It then became her mother's turn to resume the unmerciful beating. Only when her mother wearied did the punishment stop. As he walked out of the house, the father called back, "Next time when the president asks if you love Mariano, you will say Yes!"[1]

F. Eliminate Emotional Adjectives

Clearly the scene is emotionally charged. Yet I count only three emotional adjectives—defiant, uncontrollable and unmerciful. If I were writing the story today, I would eliminate unmerciful. I don't need to tell you that Luz's father was unmerciful, his actions in the story show that he was. In good story telling the emotional impact comes from the objective way in which the story is told. The effect and power of the incident would have been lost if I had tried to build up the drama of the story with more adjectives. That is called "purple prose" (i.e., highly ornamental, with too much verbiage). I would also have risked becoming maudlin.

G. Truth

1   Hugh Steven, Manuel, (Old Tappan, New Jersey, Fleming H. Revell Co. Publishers, 1970), pp 19,20.

In a poem by William Butler Yeats called "The Vision," he intoned the words, O Lord let something remain. And that is what I am interested in discovering. Is there something about the subject's life and ministry that should remain for succeeding generations to examine and ponder? Is there truth to live by? Or as J.B. Phillips said, Does the story have a ring of truth about it? Since I am concerned about the stewardship of my time, I need to ask, "What is there about this particular person's life that is significant enough for me to invest my time and emotional energy?"

1. Spiritual truth

I am also interested in what I call spiritual truth. Once again this is a personal preference and perhaps should not be considered a universal principle for storytellers. However, I have a particular interest in people who have conveyed the reality of their personal faith, not as a theoretical abstraction, but who have lived out their experience of faith in daily life. That is, I am interested in people who have walked by the truths and values they have preached or said were important to them.

2. Triumph of the Human Spirit

This doesn't mean the individual never should have failed, or that the person must display monumental faith or stoicism in the face of great adversity. On the contrary, the subject should be fully human with warts and all. But I want the subject to have displayed an inner strength and determination.

3. John Steven Aquari, 1968 Olympics in Mexico City

One example of what I mean by triumph of the human spirit occurred in the 1968 Olympics in Mexico City. Marathon runner John Steven Aquari from Tanzania had suffered a bad fall early in the marathon. Nevertheless he pushed himself through the pain of his injury to continue. When this last and almost forgotten runner limped his one remaining lap around the track, he was greeted with a standing ovation. Later when a reporter asked why, in the face of his bad injury, he didn't quit and give up, the weary and hurting athlete said with quiet dignity,

"My country didn't send me 7,000 miles to start this race. My country sent me to finish."

4. Lance Armstrong

In July 2004, the American, Lance Armstrong, stunned the sports world by winning one of the world's most grueling and celebrated sporting events, the Tour de France for an unprecedented six times. Two years before his 1999 victory, Armstrong had been fighting testicular cancer and was given only a fifty-fifty chance of survival. But through great perseverance and faith, he not only survived, but also accomplished an amazing feat of endurance by cycling 2300 miles in twenty days and beating a field of world-class cyclists by seven minutes. This is a tangible description of what I mean by truth that is spiritual. It is often difficult to define, but most recognize it when they see it. There is that "ring of truth" about it.

While it is relatively easy to spot examples of triumphs of the human spirit in sport, few of us will have the opportunity to chronicle a famous sport hero like Armstrong. This doesn't mean there are no heroes to write about. The reality is that most of the significant work being done in the Kingdom of God is being accomplished by unsung and ordinary people. Teachers, nurses, doctors, stay-at-home mothers, coaches, Sunday school teachers and more. Examine any mission agency or any community outreach ministry in any church in any country and you will find dedicated, selfless people giving of their time, talents and energy in Kingdom work. When you stir the pot and ask the right questions you will discover narratives of grace, that will amuse, challenge and inspire us all.

H. Propositional Truth or Factual Truth vs. Emotional Truth

Much of my writing for Wycliffe Bible Translators has centered on propositional truth, sometimes to the exclusion of the art and poetry in the people and events I encountered. By poetry I mean the spiritual and emotional intercommunication that occurs within the writer at both the intellectual and imaginative level. When a writer experiences deep wellsprings of emotion and feelings emerging out of his or her research or encounters with primary sources, yet omits those feelings in his or her prose, the reader, the writer and art are diminished.

Many writers who are Christians are under pressure from their organizations or their constituents to rely solely on presenting the "gospel story," or the story of their ministry in a didactic format. I believe the writer has an obligation to engage the reader intellectually and to move the reader emotionally. To do this requires an understanding of how to combine emotional and propositional or factual truth in one's prose.

1. The Taj Mahal

To record the "exact" measurements of the Taj Mahal or the Grand Canyon is one kind of truth. To be overcome by their grandeur is yet another kind of truth. Often much time is spent on factual truth, to the neglect of the beautiful or emotional truth. In an article by John Lenger from the December 1998 issue of *The Writer*, he wrote:

> Engage readers emotionally, especially if you're writing about serious things. Readers want to be your friends, to share your secrets, to laugh at your jokes, to take your side. That's why people become readers; they're looking for that emotional connection. There are two things that readers won't abide: Being preached at and being bored.

2. Monkey Bridge

Notice how this excerpt from the book *Monkey Bridge* by Vietnamese author Lan Cao touches our emotions:

> My daughter, who was born into a country already at war and sheltered in Saigon, has never known a rice field and the current of grace that runs through it like golden light. She has never known how it is farmed, how it is loved, how a bowl of rice is also a farmer's sweat, a mother's sweat. If she were to ask me, I would tell her about a rice field its beauty, the way it meanders across the land and carpets the horizon in bright emerald, the way the slate-blue water along the banks buoys the earth and

makes it float toward the sky like a carpet in flight, the way the water swallows the distant coconut palms in its depth like a permanent mirror, translucent rectangles forever framed in the very heart, the very soul of the land. To know a rice field is to know the soul of Vietnam.

I was struck by the poetic beauty and power of Lan Cao's prose and I was also rebuked. I have seen those rice fields both in Vietnam and in the Philippines and can identify with her description of their exquisite beauty. But too little of this beauty has appeared in my own prose. So consumed was I with the propositional truth of the Wycliffe story, that I often neglected to do what C.S. Lewis did in his Chronicles of Narnia. Lewis's narrative strategy was to plant a series of powerful images in the imagination of the reader and leave them there to bear their theological fruit.

3. Biography Tells What it is Like to Be Another Person

The object of biography is to convey to the reader what it's like to be a certain person, or how that person experienced his or her life. It is necessary, therefore, to convey both emotional truth as well as factual truth. I once visited the Sistine Chapel in the Vatican. If someone were writing a pure history of my visit to that famous chapel they would simply state that on a certain day at a certain time of year I visited the Sistine Chapel. That is a true fact or factual truth. But that is only one kind of truth. The other truth is how I felt as I sat in a corner by myself looking up at the most famous ceiling in the world. I was in wonderment of those magnificent paintings of prophets and the moment of creation. If I were writing my autobiography, or if someone were writing a biography of me and found that experience in my diary, that memory would reveal how I felt or experienced that event, which was one of awe and inspiration. I would want them to write about both the emotional truth as well as the factual truth.

I. This is Grammatically Correct

A British colleague once asked my help on a newsletter she was writing to her constituency. We were sitting in the courtyard of a guesthouse in

Ghana, West Africa. As I read the letter, it seemed wordy and full of "spiritual" or church language. There was little of the color and drama of what it was like to live and work in West Africa. Carefully, so as not to offend, I deleted some unnecessary words and made other editorial suggestions that included some possible anecdotes that would be of interest to her readers. In defense of keeping her original prose, my colleague replied, "But this is grammatically correct."

1. Natalie Goldberg

In her book, Writing Down the Bones, Natalie Goldberg wrote:

> I wanted my teachers to like me. I learned commas, colons, and semicolons. I wrote compositions with clear sentences that were dull and boring. Nowhere was there an original thought or genuine feeling. I was eager to give the teachers what I thought they wanted.

Let me say at once that proper spelling, punctuation and correct grammar, etc. are all important for a finished manuscript. But what I was trying to draw out from my colleague in West Africa was her deep down feelings and honest point of view. The letter was full of lifeless facts and progress reports about her work. I wanted to somehow re-ignite that tiny spark of creativity that Goldberg realized had been stifled in her own childhood because she submerged that urge in order to be well-liked. Such conformity is usually a death knell to creativity.

I wanted my colleague's collection of facts in her newsletter to glow with special warmth and to engage her reader in such a way that her constituents would know and feel what it was like to work on translation during the haramattan season when dry, dusty winds blew off the Sahara along the northwest coast of Africa getting into people's food and filling their eyes, noses and ears with gritty sand. There was nothing of such color from my colleague, only a factual report that was grammatically correct.

J. Biography is Not an Exact Science

It's vital that the biographer be as accurate as possible with his or her statistical data. At the same time, the essential feature of biography is subject to the rules of interpretation, and not everyone obeys the rules. Biography, therefore, is not an exact science. The reason is obvious. Biography deals with people, personalities and events that may have occurred fifty or a hundred years ago or more. Also, the classic definition of history is, *the memory of things said and done.* "Therefore," said one historian, "*It should be remembered that the biographer is dealing with human and moral judgments.* As such, it should not be confused with natural science."

1. Most histories (biographies) are incomplete

Most histories are incomplete because memory is fallible. Also, a biographer may have access to only fragments of information and must make judgments, even suppositions as to what might have happened. In addition, people once overlooked by historians who had either their own agenda or unrecognized biases may find new archival materials that when examined from the distance of time will reveal new insights and contributions. The celebrated disclosure in 1998, provided by the magic of DNA, reveals that Thomas Jefferson fathered at least one child by his black slave Sally Hemings.

One only has to cite histories written during the last three decades of the 20th century that have highlighted the contribution of women, blacks, Native Americans and other minorities that were overlooked by earlier historians. It was almost twenty-five years after the end of the Vietnam War that American nurses were recognized for their heroic contribution in saving and caring for so many young soldiers with their own war memorial. I share the same opinion as Archbishop James P. Lyke, of Atlanta who said, *Unless we rewrite history according to new information, we will remain imprisoned by certain cultural views that block access to the full truth of God's self-disclosures for peoples.*

2. E. H. Carr

"Great history is written," said E.H. Carr, "precisely when the historian's vision of the past is illuminated by insights into the problems of the present."[1] Carr defined history as a continuous dance between the

---

1   E. H. Carr, *What is History?* (New York, Penguin Books, 1981), p 37.

present and the past. Not only because new evidence turns up, but also because old evidence is seen in the light of new experience.

3. Stephen Ambrose

In his book *Undaunted Courage*, the story of Lewis and Clark's expedition to the Pacific Northwest in 1805-1806, Stephen Ambrose makes frequent judgments and conjectures in his narrative. Ambrose tells us that there were, *large gaps in Lewis's journal when nothing was written for days at a time.* [1] At one point Ambrose explains that Lewis had written in his journal only twice in three weeks.[2] Ambrose expresses his frustration and bewilderment over such omissions, and then fills in the gaps by surmising (based on past evidence) what might have happened. In one passage, Ambrose said, "It wasn't unusual for men of the enlightenment to write such stuff." In such circumstances, the historian admits the omission and fills in the blanks with, "I can only surmise that such and such happened." Unless one is exploring psychology, it is most unwise to invent the thoughts of an individual if you have no corroborating evidence. In my opinion, Ambrose does not cross the line of responsible biography. He covers himself by saying, "I can only surmise." The important point to notice is that *undocumented conjecture, in the story, while sometimes necessary, should always be acknowledged.*

4. Biographies Are Not Life

In order to keep a biography at readable length, the biographer can't tell everything that happened in a person's life. There must be selectivity. Thus it becomes apparent that biographies are in fact *an arrangement and an interpretation of a life and not a full life.*

K. Exercise

To give you a further example of factual truth vs. emotional truth, try describing a room in two ways. First list the objective facts that you see in the room: the number and types of chairs, pictures on the wall, the color of the carpet or lack of a carpet. After doing this, let your the emotional truth, i.e., what you feel about the room come to the surface.

1   Stephen E. Ambrose, *Undaunted Courage* (New York, Simon & Schuster, 1996), p 280.
2   *Ibid.* p 289

Chapter Seven

Biography, Part III
Do Facts Always Speak for Themselves?

The reconstruction of the past in the historian's mind is dependent upon empirical evidence. But it is not, in itself, an empirical process, and cannot consist in a mere recital of facts. On the contrary, the process of reconstruction governs the selection and interpretation of the facts: this, indeed, is what makes them historical facts.[1]

A. Facts: A Biographer's Dilemma

The dilemma has to do with facts that collide with a subject's fallibility and a biographer's idealism. Let's suppose a writer wants to write a memoir about a politician, who, in the writer's mind has made an enormous contribution to the public good. *A memoir, remember, is written by someone who personally knew the subject or by the subject himself.* Suppose the biographer approaches a story idea with a set of facts that seem to validate the original premise for the story he or she wants to tell. But when the biographer begins the research, another set of facts emerges that clashes with the original idealistic view of this particular political

---

1 E. H. Carr, *What is History?* (New York: A Pelican Book, 1981), p. 22.

figure. How do you now reconcile these two realities? This was the dilemma presidential aide to Bill Clinton, George Stephanopoulos, faced in his book, *All Too Human*. Stephanopoulos writes:

> I'm still mystified by the Clinton paradox. How could a president so intelligent, so compassionate, so public-spirited and so conscious of his place in history act in such a stupid, selfish and self-destructive manner?
>
> . . . When I first considered writing about my time with President Clinton, I envisioned a political memoir shaped like a human comedy—a story of good, talented but fallible people acting on Vaclav Havel's hope that politics cannot only be the art of the possible, It can also be the art of the impossible, namely: the art of improving ourselves and the world. I wanted to write a candid story that neither shied away from showing the "art of the possible," nor surrender to the cynical notion that there is nothing more to know about politics. I hoped to explain how an ambitious and idealistic President of uncertain personal character grew in office—how he outsmarted his enemies, out-hustled his adversaries, and achieved what no Democrat had done since Roosevelt—two full terms in office and a successful presidency. I believed it would be a story with a happy ending. But the plot took a turn.[1]

William Manchester in his book *American Caesar, Douglas MacArthur, 1880-1964* and Mark Noll in his book *Turning Points, Decisive Moments in the History of Christianity* faced what every biographer faces—how to tell the good and bad facts about their subjects in a balanced and fair way.

1. William Manchester

In describing General MacArthur, Manchester begins his book with a preamble in which he says:

---

1   George Stephanopoulos, *All Too Human*, (Boston: Little Brown and Company, 1999), p. 4.

He [MacArthur] was a great thundering paradox of a man, noble and ignoble, inspiring and outrageous, arrogant and shy, the
best of men and the worst of men, the most protean, [able to
take on a variety of shapes] most ridiculous and most sublime.
No more baffling, exasperating soldier ever wore a uniform.
Flamboyant, imperious and apocalyptic, he carried the plumage
of a flamingo, could not acknowledge errors and tried to cover
up his mistakes with sly, childish tricks. Yet he was also en-
dowed with great personal charm, a will of iron and a soaring
intellect. Unquestioningly the most gifted man-at-arms this na-
tion has produced.[1]

2. Mark Noll

Mark Noll's chapter on Martin Luther is equally honest showing both
sides to Luther's character. Noll acknowledges Luther's singular contribution to the Reformation by calling him the first Protestant. Noll holds
up Luther's linguistic genius and his celebrated translation of the Bible
into the modern understandable everyday German language. "A fact,"
Noll said, "that had greater impact in Germany than the King James Bible had in England." At the same time, Noll is bold to say that Luther
was blunt and sometimes [a] crude writer who was almost as likely to
embarrass his supporters and protectors as to edify them. Hardly to be
considered a model of Christian decorum.[2]

3. Facts, a Jigsaw Puzzle

The challenge of the biographer is to discover the essence of a person
and their ministry by sorting through the paradox of their human
strengths and weaknesses, and by examining their priorities that are often noble and ignoble. Further, the biographer must assemble the bits
and pieces of a person's life experience and then mold them into a compelling and balanced portrait that yields both enjoyment and understanding. Writing a biography, therefore, is like working one's way
through a gigantic jigsaw puzzle, with many missing pieces.

---

1   William Manchester, *American Caesar, Douglas MacArthur, 1880-1964* (New York, Dell 197,) p.15.
2   Mark A. Noll, *Turning Points, Decisive Moments in the History of Christianity* (Grand Rapids,
    Michigan: Baker Books, 1998), p. 164.

4. Uncomfortable Facts

However, as the story of a subject's life unfolds, a biographer has to decide how much to reveal. To his dismay, Stephanopoulos learned some things about President Clinton he would rather not have known. The question now becomes: Are there some facts or some kinds of information that are better for us not to know?" Roger Shattuck writing in *The American Scholar* said:

> Some information is simply not safe for us-not because there is something wrong with its possession in the abstract, but because we humans are not well suited to cope with such.[1]

(I leave this as an open-ended statement for you to ponder.) Dumas Malone who devoted his professional life to Thomas Jefferson wrote that he would have much preferred to have ignored the whole sordid question [of whether Jefferson had fathered a child with Sally Hemings] had not others the bad taste to air it.

a. Question One

The next question is axiomatic, that is: How do you handle the uncomfortable facts discovered in your research? It seems to me the biographer faces two problems. One has to do with the tension over how true he or she should be to his or her craft as an historian and reflective writer. The other question has to do with the reputation of the subject. Some biographers salivate when they discover there has been sexual misconduct, bigotry or duplicity in the life of their subject. Such scandal titillates the reader and makes for greater dramatic and literary appeal. Further, many biographers wrap themselves in the literary bromide that says, in order to achieve objectivity, all facts must be revealed to show how a person lived.

b. Warts and All

The essence of story telling has to do with showing a person working out solutions to problems by their own actions, choices and determina-

---

1   Roger Shattuck, *Forbidden Knowledge: From Prometheus To Pornography* (St. Martin's Press, from a review by Randall Curb, *To Know, or Not to Know,* in *The American Scholar,* Autumn, 1997), p.627.

tion. Readers, after all, are convinced and inspired not by exhortation, but by identification with the subject as one who has experienced the same temptations, failures and vicissitudes of life as everyone else. It's called showing the subject, "warts and all."

c. Make Value Judgments

However, I have come to believe I do not need to know absolutely everything there is to know about an individual in order to write an interpretative biography. My personal opinion is that if a biographer is writing about a person who is alive, the biographer has a duty and a courtesy to the family not to play up scandal, gossip or innuendo. The biographer should consider the possible consequences of revealing information that might damage another.

The appropriate question to ask is, "How would you feel if the roles were reversed?" The biographer should also ask if he or she can clearly and fully justify the decisions to reveal whatever it might be to the public. Finally, the decision of what to include in a biography hinges on a fundamental literary principle of story telling. Before a writer uses an anecdote or quotes a statistic or factual incident, the writer must determine if such information supports, advances and builds the story into a coherent whole.

Usually a biographer has to decide before writing what particular thesis or theme he or she wants the reader to know about the subject. In my biographies of Cameron Townsend, I wanted people to know how passionately he felt about his vision for ethnic minorities worldwide to have access to the Scriptures translated into their own languages. I also wanted to show people that Townsend was on the frontier of a grand spiritual adventure and life journey.

B. The Journey is the Story

I believe it's the journey with all its surprises, unforeseen pitfalls, twists and turns, its love interests, its suspense, danger and all its challenges for risk and choice that reveals the true essence of an individual. In a word, the journey is the story, because without the journey there could be no goal. Someone once said, "It is the quality of the journey, more than the destination that is to be celebrated." At the same time, you want the reader to have an appreciation for the person as a human being who had or has wonderful qualities as well as less than desirable aspects of his or her personality.

1. Interpret the Meaning Behind the Facts

It goes without saying that to formulate an idea, proposition, story or thesis the biographer must have access and become acquainted with the facts of a subject's life and ministry. Without such supporting facts there would be no biography. However, the biography must always go beyond the plain facts to interpret the significance or truth of what the facts reveal. While failures should be included as well as a person's successes, it is wise to understand that whatever facts you uncover, you are only beginning your story because *facts rarely exist in isolation*. This means the biographer must do more than simply gather a series of facts or generalizations. If all you have is a list of facts, then Miguel Cervantes words that "facts are an enemy of truth" apply.

2. Jane Yolen

Jane Yolen, in her book, *Guide to Writing for Children*, draws an interesting distinction between plain facts or data versus information, or what data [facts] say to us:

> If a boatman stands at the bow and shouts, "Mark twelve, mark ten, mark four," he is giving the helmsman data [facts]. But the helmsman is receiving [interpreting] the following information, "The water is getting awfully shallow, do something quick."[1]

G. Put Facts in Context of a Total Experience

The question still remains, how does a biographer overcome the barrier of bias to honestly and fairly interpret the facts of a subject's life? While admitting complete objectivity is an impossibility it doesn't mean the biographer shouldn't strive for objectivity. One way to try for objectivity is to ask yourself, "What do all the bits and pieces of the subject's life add up to?" What single message can I draw from all the facts I have gathered? Perhaps it would help to be reminded that interpretation of

1   Jane Yolen, *Guide to Writing for Children* (Boston: *The Writer, Inc.*, 1989), p. 116.

facts about an individual requires certain *integrity, knowledge, understanding, balance and a detachment on the part of the biographer.* This is particularly true when a biographer uncovers uncomfortable facts.

D. Plain Facts Do Not Always Tell the Truth

1. Gandhi

When Sir Richard Attenborough wanted to raise funds to produce the film *Gandhi*, the major studios told him, "Nobody is interested in a picture about a man dressed in a sheet." As an act of solidarity for his people and in protest over British rule, Gandhi gave up Western ways and dressed in a sheet. But the inference the studios drew from that fact was incorrect. They overlooked the man who was greater than he appeared. Here was an exceptional character that was being dismissed because some people didn't know how to interpret the facts.

2. Titanic

And what about the phenomenal success of the movie "Titanic"? Isn't this just about a big boat that hits an iceberg and sinks? Part of the story of the sinking of the Titanic is how a great ship came to an end through human arrogance-the arrogance of the Titanic's captain who ignored warnings and did not cut his speed.

3. The Open Grave

When the disciples saw the open grave three days after the death of Jesus, every fact they said in Luke 24:21 was correct:
We had hoped that he was the one who was going to redeem Israel. And what is more, it is the third day since all this took place.
The facts were correct, but the inferences the disciples drew from those facts were wrong. The new facts about the empty tomb called for a radical rearrangement of their mental furniture. For these reasons, I submit that *facts by themselves are sometimes devoid of meaning and do not always speak for themselves. Furthermore, facts can be made to mislead.*

E. Facts Are Malleable

There is an old sailing vessel story in which the captain wrote in his log, "The mate was drunk today." When the mate saw this, he added, "The captain was sober today." The assumption is that the captain's normal behavior is drunkenness. So rare was his sobriety, when it occurred it was something to be noted in the log. This, of course, is an example of a flawed warrant. It is a generalization without statistical proof or corroborating evidence that supports the mate's allegations.

Remember, facts are malleable. They can be magnified out of proportion, taken out of context, minimized or even suppressed. Further, facts are always refracted through the mind of the recorder. Two people may describe the same event in two different ways. That is to say, they do not report the fact in itself, but the fact as they saw it. When I asked my linguist and lawyer son, Lee Steven, to comment on my reasoning about facts, he said:

> Facts are data points and tell us little without interpretation, context and integration. Facts alone are like words in a language. In isolation they have an abstract meaning, usually more than one meaning. Only when words are integrated into a wider field of syntax and discourse do they take on specific meaning—and even then they are often subject to multiple interpretations.

Facts, therefore, must not only be interpreted, they must be tested to see whether they fit the data of the case in question and whether, at the same time, they agree with the accepted knowledge of an individual. This process is also true when it comes to examining primary documents. Diaries, journals, letters, interview notes and newsletters are all excellent sources of information and documentation. However, I must also say that while documents are indispensable to the historian, be aware of E.H. Carr's reminder:

Documents do not always tell what may have happened, only what the chronicler wanted others to think, or perhaps what he wanted himself to think or believe.[1]

1. The Biographer As Detective

A key word for the biographer is *finding,* as in finding the essence of your subject through research. The similarity between an historian and a detective is obvious. Both interview people from a variety of life situations. Both collect seemingly routine bits of trivia and memorabilia in an effort to determine the essence and character of an individual. Like a detective, the biographer compares conflicting bits of information to see which facts are overriding, what are dominant, and what truth the dominant facts add up to. Then from the raw data, the biographer, like the detective, looks for facts that will reveal the significance and essence of a person's life and work.

2. Test Theories Against Evidence

It is for this reason that you must test theories against evidence. Most often the biographer draws inferences from a widely diverse range of sources. Some of the information will come from people who are eager to tell you all they know. Others may have their own agenda, and in fact, be uncooperative. Or they may deliberately suppress facts that would contribute to a greater understanding of the individual.

3. Check and Recheck Your Facts

Some of the more uncomfortable moments for a biographer occur when the research reveals potential damaging facts. When that happens, it is incumbent upon the biographer to double check information to make certain the facts are indeed true facts. This forces the biographer to analyze the facts to decide what they mean in context. The way to do this is to think through the implications to see what pattern and shape the facts take. At this point the biographer combines the art of the *novelist, the detective work of the historian and the insights of a psychologist.*

---

1   *Ibid.* p. 19.

4. No Life can be fully known

This point is worth repeating: *the historian never has access to all the facts.* And because the biographer is never omniscient, *no life can be recaptured wholly as it was lived.* When you gather facts for your biography it is important to remember that you are working with a highly condensed summary of a particular occurrence. Much to my chagrin, I have learned that no matter how diligent I thought I was in collecting facts about a person's life, I have invariably missed or overlooked an important segment of my subject's life. You will save yourself a great deal of stress if you understand that no life can ever be fully known. At best the biographer can only give a perspective, or in some cases a cameo of an individual.

For many years I felt compelled to write what I thought should be the definitive portrait of an individual. This put me under a great deal of unnecessary pressure and stress. I then discovered that no one historian could examine everything from all points of view. The reason is that the Heisenberg Principle takes over, namely, *the more accurately you measure one dimension in life, the more fully another escapes you.* [1]

5. Colin Brown

Colin Brown, in his book *History and Faith*, helped me understand that not all the facts I gathered had to be used nor did I have to tell the whole story of a person's life and ministry:

> The most any [biographer] can do is to look at his or her subject in relation to certain questions. The historian then has to leave it for others [or come back to the subject] to bring out other aspects of the subject's life. [2]

F. Not All Facts are Equally Important

If there is a man who walks around your neighborhood dressed in a sheet he may be considered odd and eccentric. However, unless we are talking about a person who, like Gandhi, left an indelible trace in his-

---

1   Stacy Schriff, *Perpendicular Lives* (Washington, D. C., The American Scholar, Spring, 1999), p.   54
2   Colin Brown, *History and Faith, A Personal Exploration* (Grand Rapids: Zondervan Publishing House, 1987), p. 55.

tory, his dress preference is of no consequence to history. Thus there are past facts that have been forgotten immediately because they have no meaning. They are in history, but are not historical. I vacationed in Spain, I was a June bride, and I went to the dentist. These facts exist, but they do not have any special meaning unless, of course, a trip to the dentist in some way resulted in a life-changing event. And in Gandhi's case, the sheet became, like the man himself, a symbol that was greater than the sum of its parts.

1. When Are Facts Historical?

Facts then become historical when they are interpreted and give meaning and shape to human experience. *An historical event always leaves a trace in the memory of the person or group.* Most people of a certain age remember what they were doing when they heard the news that Pearl Harbor was bombed, or when JFK was assassinated, when Neil Armstrong first walked on the moon, when Princess Diana was killed, or where they were on 9/11/2001. There are, of course, facts that count as historical in the lives of ordinary people. Many point to pivotal or defining moments in their lives. A marriage, the birth of a first child, religious conversion, death of a parent, a major move to a new city. Since most of us will write about "ordinary people," these facts and the meaning behind each of these facts become the building blocks of your story.

G. Objectivity

One of the biggest challenges facing any biographer who wants to put the facts of a person's life into a coherent whole is objectivity. Yet every writer knows that complete objectivity is impossibility. Everyone has prejudices. The fact that I am a Caucasian male, born and raised in western Canada automatically gives me a certain bias. In an age of political correctness I am almost embarrassed with these facts. However, I have come to the conclusion that my historic and cultural background gives a certain texture to my worldview that is unique. This, of course, is true of every human being.

1. Diego Rivera

Diego Rivera, one of the great artists of the twentieth century (1867-1957) said, *the secret of my work (talent) is that it is Mexican.* Most people seem to live on the outer margins of history, but not Diego Rivera. He was aware of his singularity and place in history. As such, he was able to paint from deep inside his Mexican soul and culture. He was a person who knew who he was and who he was not. And this I believe is what is required of all writers. That is, writers should be aware of who and what they are. More important, they should be aware of what they are not. The reason is that truth in art, if it is to endure, has, as Einstein said, to stand the test of experience.

2. C.S. Lewis

In a fundamental sense your work will reflect the essence of what and who you are. C.S. Lewis once said: "Whatever spiritual roots you have struck will come out all unbidden in your work." And this is the reality you look for among the facts of your subject's life.

H. Give Credit to the Sources of Your Facts

Biographers who want to be taken seriously must be careful about giving accurate credit to their sources of fact. All writers use material (as I have done throughout this book) from a variety of sources. I am always pleased to use material that lends support to my own ideas. And I am happy also to have the reader distinguish my ideas from those of others. It's therefore vital to give credit in the footnotes and in your text to where your ideas originated.

There is another fundamental reason for giving credit to your source material. It is ethical. If you copy verbatim or almost verbatim a work and claim it as your own, that is plagiarism. If you are not careful to give specific credit to the source of your facts, editors and others will soon come to discount and distrust your work.

1. Use Primary Sources

I once made a serious mistake of using as the basis of an article a press release written by a colleague relating the part a translation team played in a serious earthquake in Peru. After the article was published, the translator wrote to tell me I was incorrect on several points. I wrote back, apologized for my errors and explained that I had gotten most of my statistical information from an internal report written by such-and-such a person. About a year after that incident I was in a meeting where this person was speaking. To my amazement he spoke about the report he had written and volunteered that to make the article more exciting he made some of the events and the part the translators played in the earthquake more dramatic than they actually were. That taught me a valuable research lesson about the importance of using only primary source material when you are writing a story for posterity. It also taught me to always give credit to the source from which I obtained the information. One of my mistakes was not verifying my facts with someone who had been directly involved with the story. And most important of all, prior to publication I should have sent the translator my article for approval. And here is the major difference between biography and fiction.

2. Don't Invent the Plot

The fiction writer can, if he or she wishes, invent the danger, threat, crises and the obstacles the hero has to overcome. In a word, the fiction writer can invent the plot. On the other hand, the biographer, while using the techniques of the fiction writer, i.e., plotting, suspense, dramatic conflict and character development, must deal with facts that cannot be changed. The biographer must never go beyond the facts that have been discovered through research.

I. Evaluate Your Facts

Finally, biographers should assess their facts by asking themselves: (a) what do all these bits and pieces of information add up to? (b) What single message do the facts reveal that would be important or helpful for the reader? (c) Would your character be damaged by using some of the facts you discovered in your research?

(d) How can you take the well-worn facts and information and create a fresh, new and vibrant story? (e) How should the story be constructed? What should come first, what next? What should be used, what should be left out?

Chapter Eight

Interviewing: A Road to Discovery

A. Be Prepared

The art of asking questions, or interviewing, is the traditional way for writers to begin building an intelligent, integrated portrait of their subject. However, in order to create such a portrait the biographer must first know how to ask the right kind of questions. (*The answers you get will depend on the kinds of questions you ask*). That means doing homework, research and preparation of well-thought-out questions before the interview.

I once read about a reporter who was supposed to have asked Vivien Leigh at the premier of the reissue of *Gone With the Wind* what part she played in the film. The response from Vivien Leigh, who played the part of Scarlet O'Hara, was that she did not care to be interviewed by such an ignoramus. This may be apocryphal, but the truth it teaches is axiomatic, namely, that the most important part of the interview, so far as the questioner is concerned, takes place before the interview. Doing homework allows the writer time to avoid the uninformed question. If your subject is a scholar or a public figure, it is wise to have read some of their published works, including quotes and articles from newspapers, journals and monograms.

B. What If You Don't Have Time to Do Your Homework?

There have been occasions when I have been asked to write a feature profile article for whom there was little time to do adequate research. When that happens, I try to interview the subject on their home turf.

1. Small Talk

Generally when you first meet your subject there is a period of small talk. That's when the observant interviewer can pick up on subtle, or not so subtle habits, offbeat interests and hobbies. Observing the subject's artifacts, bric-a-brac, photos, books, paintings, awards, etc., on display in the person's home or office can reveal a great deal about the subject.

In the office of one subject, I noticed a series of different lighthouses. When I commented on them, the woman said that both she and her husband were avid collectors of photos and painting of lighthouses. After a few leading questions I learned the couple not only collected paintings and photographs of lighthouses because they found them aesthetically pleasing, but they also held a symbolic meaning. The couples were investment brokers and wanted to provide financial "light" and investment "safety" for their customers. The lighthouse was a metaphor for their business ethic. And because of my interest in her hobby the woman was happy to tell me about lighthouses, and was open to discussing other issues unrelated to lighthouses.

C. Build Rapport, and Begin Slowly.

If the first rule of interviewing is research, the second has to be to *build rapport, create and maintain a trustful, cordial atmosphere.* The task of the interviewer is to be an icebreaker, to slowly relieve tension and to create a safe, warm, empathetic atmosphere. The ideal interview should have the feel of a good conversation with warmth, acceptance and where the subject talks, rather than simply answers questions. The object is to keep the conversation moving without the interviewer monopolizing the conversation. The death knell for any interview is when the interviewer talks more than the subject.

D. Be Flexible and Begin With Your Subject's Most Immediate Interest

While an interviewer should have a series of well thought out questions going into an interview, the interviewer shouldn't be bound by a strict mechanical set of interview procedures. Be flexible and open to changing your interview strategy. Every interview has its own unique texture and dynamic. On one occasion I was taken to the greenhouse of a man who was potting his prize fuchsias. I was unaware of this man's hobby, and knew absolutely nothing about growing fuchsias, but that's where I began the interview. We ended up sitting on the patio surrounded by a variety of his prize-winning fuchsia plants in full bloom.

E. Avoid the Word "Interview"

I believe most people like to be singled out for their opinions or asked questions about their grandchildren, hobbies or vacation trips. However, they may be apprehensive about the idea of a serious formal in-depth interview. For this reason I try to avoid the word "interview." I might say something like, "I would be interested in learning about how you chose your career." Or, "Tell me what it was like to climb Mt. Kilimanjaro? Or, Why did you drop out of college and join the Peace Corps?" To avoid yes and no answers I ask open-ended questions by using "how" and "why" words.

1. Location

Some of my interviews have occurred in a restaurant over lunch. If you are tape-recording the interview (as I always do), interviewing in a restaurant has the problem of background noise. My preference is to interview a person in a place where they feel at ease and where they won't be interrupted. If you must interview in a restaurant, look for a quiet corner and seat the subject so that his or her back is to oncoming traffic, e.g., waiters and such.

Just a note about interview manners of a writer, it is always wise to observe correct social protocol. If you are in the subject's home or office, wait to be invited to sit down and let the subject be the one to move toward informality. I am also aware the interviewer might be sitting for a long time. While it is important to be comfortable, the interviewer should avoid becoming too comfortable. I don't want to doze off in the middle of a long interview. For this reason I prefer a straight-back chair. In this way I can maintain eye contact, and by word and gesture indicate that I am on track with the subject's story. While I am recording the interview, I also have a steno pad on my lap where I can note specific questions, or points of clarification I may want to ask later. I am, of course, speaking about interviewing people for longer book projects. However, if you are interviewing a person for a shorter magazine article you essentially want to create the same kind of bond and empathetic interest as you do for a longer project, time constraints not withstanding.

F. Hurdles

In any investigation, the interviewer can encounter a number of unforeseen hurdles. The first is to get the interviewer talking freely enough to tell you the anecdotes, quotes, facts and color that will make for a compelling and interesting story. Assuming the interviewer has done his or her homework and prepared well, the interview can still be a journey into dangerous territory.

1. Painful Memories

The reason a biographer may find the terrain difficult is because both the subject and the interviewer (although the interviewee may not recognize it at first) are on a road to discovery. It can be a discovery that sometimes brings the subject face-to-face with revelations that he or she would rather not discuss or, may in fact, never knew existed. Invariably in any in-depth interview there are painful memories of past experiences that have been covered up and locked away. The trauma that Elie Wiesel (Author of *Night*) went through during his imprisonment in Buchenwald and Auschwitz resulted in a ten-year vow of silence before describing what happened during that awful time.

2. Tears

When I interviewed a couple whose two-year-old daughter had died on the operating table several years prior to my interview, I knew reliving that memory would be painful for the parents. I also knew I needed the details since the incident was pivotal to the story. For the first hour or so the interview went well. Each parent supplied anecdotes of their childhood, career, courtship, marriage and the birth of their children. Then without warning, the mother erupted into a gusher of sobs and tears. Her sense memory associated with the hurt and pain that came from reliving the death of her daughter overwhelmed her. For some minutes she was inconsolable. When the dam of emotion was spent, the mother told me how she felt when she learned of her daughter's death:

> Feeling utterly alone I walked out of the hospital waiting room and into the hospital parking lot (my husband was making funeral arrangements). When I came to our car I rested my hand on the door handle and looked up into a beautiful blue Alaska sky that was sharp and clear. As I opened the door and slid into the seat I said to myself, 'It's a myth, there isn't any God. He doesn't exist. I've been fed a pack of lies. There is no one up there.' But no sooner had I given vent to my feelings of grief and anger than I seemed to hear a gentle voice in my heart that said, *Have confidence, Child, I am still here.* [1]

G. Pretending Not to Hear

Another bit of dangerous territory can come from the uncooperative person who either has an agenda, or for some bizarre reason feeds you incorrect or highly biased information. Most often such people are secondary sources (family, friends, colleagues) whom you are interviewing for a fuller and more comprehensive picture of the principal subject. I have also encountered people who maintained a superficial attitude and were unwilling to comment on specific concrete details. They spoke only in generalities. In several cases I was unable to write either the kind of story I felt should have been told, or any story at all.

---

1 Hugh Steven, *Good Broth to Warm Our Bones*, (Westchester, Illinois, Crossway Books, 1982), p. 157.

1. Primary Sources

For this reason I agree with Barbara Tuchman who said she depended primarily on first-hand or primary sources and accounts and treated second-hand (other authors' commentaries) "very gingerly." To be fair, there are some secondary, and primary sources that have legitimate reasons for refusing to be interviewed. If I have an important source that chooses not to be interviewed, I will often do the research without their input. After concluding my work I will again contact the person and tell them I have completed my research and have drawn certain conclusions. I then ask if they would like to read my draft, or I tell them what I had found. If they agree to listen or read my copy, I invite them to suggest any further comments or insights. Often the once-reluctant secondary source is only too happy to correct my presuppositions or to give me an insight I had overlooked.

H. How Do I Know If The Story is Correct?

The question still remains, how do I know if what I am hearing is correct? The answer is, I don't always know. For this reason I interview several different sources. When I begin to have different sources corroborating my facts and telling similar anecdotes about my subject, I then feel about ready to write the story. Also, when I am interviewing, I am careful to observe the individual's body language.

I. Body Language and Being an Attentive Listener

In the adventures of the *Cardboard Box*, Sherlock Holmes says to Dr. Watson:

> You remember, said he, that some little time ago when I read you the passage in one of Poe's sketches in which a close reasoned follows the unspoken thoughts of his companion you were inclined to treat the matter as a mere tour-de-force of the author. On my remarking that I was constantly in the habit of doing the same thing you expressed incredulity. "Oh no," [you

said]. Perhaps not with your tongue, my dear Watson, but certainly with your eyebrows.[1]

Every culture has its own unique body language. Western American culture admires the direct verbal attack. Not so the Japanese. They usually avoid the direct question. The Japanese language contains many vague phrases that are designed to camouflage one's true inner feelings. When two Americans talk together they are likely to end a statement with a drop of the head, or lowering of the eyelids. In Canada, the end of a statement usually ended with an up-glide that almost sounds like a question. Similarly the English wind up a question with a lift of the hand, tilt of the chin or a widening of the eyes. With a future tense verb they often gesture with a forward movement.

Since we communicate with one another nonverbally as well as with words, I want the person I am interviewing to know by my body language, my gestures, the inflection and tone of my voice, eye contact and an engaged body position (usually leaning forward, with uncrossed arms) that I am genuinely interested in their story and in them as an individual. In a word, I want to be fully present to the subject.

Being a good listener means bending your mind, to listen sensitively and carefully to what the subject is saying since much of a person's body language is subconscious or subliminal; the astute interviewer is alert to discrepancies between what a person says and how they say it. A man who says to a woman, "I love you," is using a grammatical utterance to convey an attitude. The intelligent and wise woman hearing such a sentiment will pay more attention to the accompanying Para-language or vocal phenomena. This consists of such things a pitch, intensity, stress tempo and volume or simple intonation.

In his book, *Language in Thought* and Action S.I. Hayakawa says:

> The quality of the voice itself has the power of expressing feelings that are almost independent of the symbols used. We can say, 'I hope you come back and see us again,' in such a way that clearly indicates that we hope the visitor never comes back. Or again, if the young lady with whom we are strolling says, 'The moon is bright tonight,' we are able to tell by the tone whether

---

1   Sir Arthur Conan Doyle, *The Complete Sherlock Holmes* (New York: Doubleday, 1927) pp. 888, 889

she is making a meteorological observation or indicating that she wants to be kissed.[1]

J. A Nostalgic Frame of Mind

How do you interview the person who says, as one person once said to me, "I have absolutely no recollection of my childhood, and not much memory for what happened last year." To jump-start a person's memory I often try to move the subject to a nostalgic frame of mind. That is, I use brief words and phrases from their past that I hope will bring feelings to the surface of their remembrance. For example you might ask the person if they ever had a dog or another pet. Then ask its name. Or, you might ask if the person remembers their first car. Curiously, the person who was most adamant that she couldn't remember anything about her youth, waxed passionate about her first car. "It was a red roadster that drove like a dream."

1. Selective Memories

Some people have psychological reasons for not being able to remember something or remember it accurately. Often the conclusions we draw from a set of facts lead us to change the facts themselves. This is not intentional but it is nearly universal, which is why a good researcher must always check the facts they have been told against documents or other evidence.

A perfect example of this was the celebrated case before the United States Congress where a dozen chief executives from the big tobacco industry testified under oath that cigarettes were not addictive, nor were they adding nicotine to make smokers more dependent on their product. We now know the executives lied, or did not tell the truth or were themselves duped. The reality is that a CEO who is being paid a six-figure salary plus lucrative stock options will never speak against his own self-interest.

It goes without saying that how people see the world or things in the world will depend in part upon external objective reality. In the case of the CEOs, the objective reality was their position of power and huge salaries. The CEOs testimony was based upon individual needs, goals,

---

1   S. I. Hayakawa, *Language in Thought and Action* (London, George Allen & Unwin LTD, 1966), p. 70.

motives and past experiences. Thus you know before going into such an interview what the outcome will be. No CEO from a Tobacco Company will give you an objective, unbiased opinion as to the health hazards of smoking.

K. Practical Tips for Conducting an Interview

1. Credit Card Information or Building a Dossier

"Accuracy," said A.E. Housman, "is a duty, not a virtue." Accurate quotes and verifiable sources correctly footnoted are indispensable to good scholarship. When you begin to interview or research your subject, the *credit card* information about your subject is most important. That is, accurate statistical or factual information about the individual. Such data includes birth date, childhood, schooling, graduations, marriage, careers, outstanding achievements, reading habits, name and ages of children, hobbies, career awards, where the person lived at certain times in their history, etc. While this is an important first step in writing a biography, such detailed facts do not make a story, any more than a bank security camera creates a film. In reality, all you have at this point is an objective recipe list, the kind you might find in an encyclopedia.

L. The Differences and Similarities Between Journalism and Biography

If you are trained as an objective journalist, you do indeed find your story ready-made in the objective facts. The journalist's role is to collect facts and edit materials of current interest for presentation through a news media. Generally, a journalist presents the facts or description of events without attempting to interpret the events or facts. The stories a journalist writes are generally objective, factual, uninvolved, that is, the journalist hasn't taken a position or championed a particular cause.

M. Who, What Where, When, and How

The biographer, on the other hand is a person who must trace an individual's life through all of its intricate developments. And this requires hard, labor-intensive work and imagination. One trusty method to help the writer on this road to discovery comes from the world of journalism where reporters want to know the answers to: who, what, where, when and how. That is, when interviewing for a story ask yourself:

1. What happened?
2. Who took part?
3. When did it happen?
4. Where did it happen?
5. Why did this event (or these events) take place?
6. How did it happen?

1. Getting At the Essence of Your Subject

You ask these questions to discover the essence of your subject. To get your central character clearly defined in your mind you want to discover what it is that makes that person unique. You also want to know what are, or were, the experiences that produced these interesting and unique qualities. Peter Jacobi in an article in *The Writer's 1990 Year Book* gives what in my mind is some of the best interviewing advice:

> Your questions have to be as creative as any piece of writing you will do—bold, probing, yet tactful. You must stay with the interview, persevering until the questions are answered fully and until they honestly illuminate major issues and personality traits. You need to recognize and deal promptly with sidestepping responses, half-truths, braggadocio, and even outright prevarication. And you must arrange the questioning so that an integrated picture of the subject emerges, mosaic-like, rather than in random disconnected bursts of insight or confidence.[1]

N. The Historical Perspective

A basic principle of New Testament biblical exegesis is to have an appreciation and understanding of the historical context out of which the narrative stories, letters, and poetry, etc. were written. This means understanding something about the people who lived and worked in the Greco-Roman world. So too, does the biographer need to know as much as possible about their character's geographical world, the times in which he or she lived as well as the person's world view, preoccupa-

---

1   Peter P. Jacobi, *Writing the Personality Profile*, (The Writer's 1990 Year Book), pp. 27,28.

tions and motivations. Part of my own interview procedure is to physically visit the place or places where my subject lived and worked. I like to breathe the same air, walk the same streets in the neighborhood where the subject grew up. I like to visit the subject's house, school, church and work place.

1. Good Broth to Warm Our Bones

When I researched the book *Good Broth to Warm Our Bones*, a story that takes place among the *Inupiat* of Alaska, I spent time in Barrow, Alaska and entered into the daily ebb and flow of the small community. I walked out on the ice floes, fished for tom cod through leads in the ice, visited the homes of old-timers, smelled the barrels of seal oil in their kitchens, ate muktuk (whale blubber), spent time with people in coffee shops. I visited the local museum and Senior Citizens Center, the post office and supermarket. (To my surprise, I discovered the inhabitants of Barrow consume vastly more Coke and Pepsi per capita than do people in all of the lower forty-eight). I read everything I could find about Eskimo Inupiat lifestyles. I wanted to know as much as possible about Inupiat hunting methods, early family histories, weather reports, tide shifts. It turned out that a wind and tide shift played a critical role in the life of one of the main characters. Someone once said:

> Research is a fascinating combination of hunches, speculation, subjectivity, imagination, hopes and dreams blended precisely with objectively gathered facts tied down to the reality of a mathematical science. One without the other is incomplete. Together they inch along the road, wherever it may be found.

O. A Personal Objective

One of my personal objectives in interviewing is to discover what, in the routine of life, raising children, preparing meals, doing laundry, getting up each day and going to work gives an individual focus, or unity in the choices and decisions he or she makes. If life is, as someone has described, merely a collection of moments, then I want to know what it is that unites these moments and gives them coherence and purpose.

P. No Rules for Interviewing

On the other hand, some writers deliberately avoid asking specific questions. Rather, they just say, "Tell me what it's like to go scuba diving in the Bahamas." Alex Haley, author of *Roots* and *Malcom X* said for him there were no rules for interviewing he just used all the things he could think of from his own experience.

Q. Transcribe Your Own Notes

I want to stress the importance of transcribing one's personal field notes. Voice inflections, pregnant pauses, and evasions can often tell you more than the verbal stream. After I have transcribed my notes and organized my second set of questions, I ask for another interview. (I always inform my subject that it will usually take two or three interview sessions to get the complete story. The last two interviews will be much shorter than the first interview; sometimes all that is needed is a phone call to clarify a certain point. In most cases the first interview provides a skeleton outline of how the story might develop. If you are writing an authorized biography, as I was in writing on the life and times of the founder of Wycliffe Bible Translators, William Cameron Townsend, I had access to all archival papers. (I requested that all the relevant material be photocopied. Exact copies of handwritten letters, notes and diaries have a way of quickening the biographer's literary juices long after one's field notes have grown cold.)

When you examine a person's letters, papers, diaries, scribbling, artifacts, photos and other items an individual has saved over the years, not all will be equally useful. But they become important vehicles for giving insights into the essence and psychological makeup of your subject. They often reveal wonderful eccentricities that add color to your story.

U. When Do You Know When You Have Done Enough Research?

By nature I am an explorer. I love to learn, to gain fresh insight into the human comedy, besides, it's easier than writing. There is, however, the distinct danger of using research to delay the day when you switch gears from objective observer, to a reflective author. Once again, the best advice I can offer on when to stop doing research is taken from Barbara Tuchman's book *Practicing History*, a book I highly recommend:

The most important thing about research is to know when to stop. When I was eighteen or thereabout, my mother told me that when I went out with a young man I should always leave a half-hour before I wanted to. Although I was not sure how this might be accomplished, the advice is sound, and exactly the same rule applies to research. One must stop before one has finished, otherwise, one will never stop and never finish.[1]

---

1   Barbara W. Tuchman, *Selected Essays Practicing History* (New York, Ballantine Books, 1981), p. 20.

Chapter Nine

Journaling

W*rite in a book for yourself all the words that I have spoken to you (for human memory might soon forget them) (Jeremiah: 30:2).*

A. A Postcard Before Dying

My friend George stopped me in the church parking lot one Sunday morning. "Can you recommend a book on journaling? It's for my wife Esther," He said. "We're not certain how long she has to live. The cancer has spread throughout her body. She has some good days and some bad. With the strength she has on her good days she would like to keep a journal of what she is learning and experiencing of God's grace and strength through this last stage of her life, or, as she says, 'On her journey to a new land.' Esther would also like to mail postcards to friends and family based on her jottings from her journal. Do you have any ideas, or suggestions about how she can do this?"

At the time, I was working on this very chapter and decided to send Esther a distillation of my thoughts and those of others on the nature of journaling.

Dear Esther,

The literary world knows a good deal about the life and times of people like George Washington, John Adams, Henry David Thoreau, Anne Frank, Dag Hammarskjold, John Wesley, Queen Victoria, Amy Carmichael, Jim Elliot, Lewis and Clark and hundreds of others all because they kept diaries and personal journals of their daily life experiences. John Wesley, for example, began his diary during his student days at Oxford. His aim in keeping his diary was "to profess, edify, reform and inspire."

Esther, there are as many reasons why people journal as there are ways and methods of keeping one. George told me you wanted to keep a journal in preparation for your personal journey to a "new land." Interestingly, there is a direct correlation between journaling and going on a journey. I don't necessarily mean physically traveling, although that is a popular reason why people journal. In a unique way each day of our lives is a kind of journey. Certainly our daily spiritual life with God is a journey of faith. Each person's life is a kind of scripture waiting to be read and interpreted as a sacred text that is capable of revealing divine truth when seen through the eyes of faith.

The journal of Amy Carmichael, who was bedridden for the last twenty years of her life, reveals that she journeyed farther and gained greater insight and self-knowledge as she moved closer to God through her affliction.

B. A Journal Can Pinpoint Special and Pivotal Moments

Like Amy Carmichael or Anne Frank you Esther, now have time to explore your feelings about what is happening to you. In a thoughtful reflective way, you can clarify what is and has been vital in your life and what has been trivial and not worth worrying about. This will be a special treasure and wonderful legacy for your family and friends. The following are some clues to help you discover the nourishment and wisdom that can come from reflective journaling.

C. Your Journal is a Special Friend

Many people look upon their journal as a special friend. Anne Frank addressed each entry to, "Dear Kitty." A journal thus becomes a sounding board, a place where one can clarify thoughts and feelings. Others use their journal to record the pivotal moments that made a significant difference in their lives. One famous diarist wrote: *My journal keeps open house to every kind of happening in my soul. My journal is my super-confidante."*

D. How to Journal

Since I consider legalism to be a deterrent to creativity, I don't always journal every day. However, when I do, I start by recording the day of the week, date and time of day.

1. Eschew Laundry Lists

Rather than record a laundry list of things that happened on a certain day, I record the most significant event of my life at that moment in good times or bad, sad or joyful. For example, on one occasion, the person whose life history I was chronicling rejected the manuscript I had worked on for many months. It was a bitter and painful moment, partly because of the way I was informed. In my journal I wrote:

Today is Monday April 29/85. This has been a difficult, yet important past three days. It all began with an unkind letter from . . . A hard letter to receive about the book. But the Lord is gracious. I want to affirm the truth of Psalm 37:1 *Don't fret, trust in the Lord. Commit your way to the Lord. Be still and know that I am the Lord, wait patiently and refrain from anger and turn from wrath, do not fret— it only leads to evil.*

The message from the Lord that morning was loud and clear, namely, that I should be still, patient, kind, good to others and to relax and delight myself in God. On May 28 I began work on another book that was later published and became an important outreach tool for Wycliffe Associates. When I looked back and read my journal for those difficult weeks, the pain of rejection returns. Yet there is great praise to God for His faithfulness. When I shared my pain of the first book being "dead in the water" to a friend, he wrote back and said, Read Isaiah 64:4: *For since the world began no one has seen or heard of such a God as ours who works for those who wait for Him.*

I wrote that response underneath my April 29 journal entry. That event had become a living reminder that God does indeed work on behalf of His children. The lesson, of course, is that the truth and blessing of that episode in my life would have been lost forever if I hadn't taken the time to record it in my journal.

E. Be Spontaneous, Be Yourself

It's helpful to remember that journaling is like talking to an intimate, longtime friend. You don't have to wear a mask. You are writing for yourself and can therefore be yourself, free from all pretense and inhibition. You don't have to worry or be concerned about sentence length, grammar or spelling. Luci Shaw said:

> You are journaling for personal illumination, recording your own thoughts and observation for your own edification and growth.[1]

F. Tools

In her book *Life Path*, Luci Shaw says that choosing the right notebook, (size, binding, lined or blank pages) can affect the way you write. I found that a small notebook not only cramped my handwriting but my style as well. Whenever I take a major trip I begin a new journal in a lined inexpensive 6x8-inch notebook or steno pad with a spiral back that opens flat.

---

1   Luci Shaw, *Life Path, Personal Growth Through Journal Writing*, Multnomah Press Portland, Oregon 1991) p. 39.

G. The Travel Journal

In my role as writer/photographer I usually travel alone, except that I have my journal, which becomes a familiar friend and traveling companion. I keep my journal in my camera bag ready to record my feelings and observations whenever I have a spare moment. One of my favorite places to write is in a restaurant while waiting for a meal. Another favorite place is in an airport-waiting lounge.

Along with events I experienced, including people I meet, I record bits of overheard conversations, newspaper headlines, songs I heard and how the music affected me. At a later date these will become "trigger" words that help me recall the specific event.

In addition to the photos I take, I sometimes make crude (I am not artist) sketches, of the land or other objects. I might paste in a menu, a bus or train timetable, or ticket stub. At a future date I evaluate my experience. The critical thing is that my journal becomes a repository of emotions and observations that allows me to recall what I was doing and how I felt at a specific moment in time. These journal entries will becomes the raw material or the foundation from which I will later build my books and articles.

H. Take a Cue from the Psalms

Esther, you might be experiencing new emotions that our Christian sub-culture has taught us to repress. The reality is that God knows all about your emotions. We can't hide them from Him. Whenever I become depressed, angry or frustrated, I take a cue from King David who poured out his soul before God in the Psalms. Many of David's Psalms are full of anger, frustration, disappointment, grief, longings, as well as moments of ecstatic joy and praise for answered prayer. Clearly the Psalms were David's journal. For David, poetry was a way of releasing his emotional burdens and dealing with his stress. You too might find writing some free verse poetry helpful.

I. Revisit your Journal

After you have recorded your feelings and responses to life on a particular day, you might find it helpful to go back a day or so later and revise, soften or add to what you had written. The passage of a day or so may allow one to gain a new perspective on a situation.

J. Postscript

Esther died a week after I sent my letter. When I heard the news I felt bad that I hadn't gotten this information to her sooner. But at her funeral her pastor read the following postcard from her journal written just days before she died:

> George has set up a hospital bed in the living room. I love it! I couldn't imagine a better place to die. From my bed I can look out double French doors at a sunny deck, a large bubbling fountain and a beautiful flower garden. I enjoy phone calls and visits from friends and family. So far, I've been able to get out of bed and into a wheelchair. I enjoy the sun as I sit on the deck and get wheeled around the backyard by one of my sons.
>
> George has hired some help to provide care and companionship through the day and early evening. My morning routine includes using my walker to walk around my bedroom to feed my fish, check my social calendar and occasionally step on the scale for a weight check. (Cancer is one heck of a weight-loss program!) But I have to admit, most of my time is spent lying in bed enjoying God's Spirit, talking to my Heavenly Father and dealing with my various discomforts. I use medication to manage my pain. It is supplied through a patch. Sometimes I take pills for added punch. But I am doing all right. I have lots of moments of peace and calm. Most of all, I have an overwhelming sense of closeness with God. This is what I want to share. Only God knows how long any of us has here. From time to time I'll send you a postcard sharing the highlights of my journey to a New Land. In the meantime Hebrews 13:14 and John 14:1-3 are a great comfort.

K. Musings From My Journal

To illustrate the importance of recording concrete details in your journal, allow me to share three musings from my personal journal. The first became a chapter in my book *Behind the Story* under the title *Six Flies, and Warm Apple Pop*. The first incident occurred one hot muggy morning in a small town in Southern Mexico. I had a few hours to spare before my plane left for Mexico City. Hungry, hot and thirsty, I walked into a "hole-in-the-wall" restaurant across the street from the town's bus terminal:

> As I sit down, I am immediately aware of my table. It's a simple rough-cut pine table with square untapered legs. One leg is shorter than the others. The table wobbles. I am also aware of my chrome chair. The seat is covered with a heavy clear plastic and it has several tears, all of which are repaired with the miracle product, Scotch Tape. My table is covered with a sticky plastic tablecloth. Six flies flit back and forth between my table and the opposite chair.
>
> I next notice the painted walls of this high-ceiling restaurant. It's a kind of faded blue-purple with dull canary-yellow wooden shutters on windows that are open to the street. A single overhead fan tries in vain to dissipate the rising humidity and heat that is beginning to seep through the open windows and doorway. At a table near mine sit four rumpled men who look as if they had slept in their clothes. All sport Arafat beards. One rubs the sleep from his eyes. The others sit silently staring into space.
>
> My host for the moment is a timid young man of about fourteen or fifteen. I ask for the menu. "All we have are drinks," he says. I remind him there are some eggs sitting in a basket on the counter. "Oh yes," he says. "We can give you scrambled eggs mixed with Spanish sausage or ham." I choose the ham.

As the young man shuffles away to give the cook my order, I examine more closely just how this restaurant operates. I conclude it is a family operation with the mother orchestrating the events. She makes change out of her purse that sits on top of an old ornate cash register, the kind that has a hand-crank on the side. Her instructions to the table boy and cook are given without a smile and with the intensity of a captain of industry.

Behind the counter is her six-, or seven-, maybe even eight-year old daughter. She wears a flower-print dress and rests her chin on the counter. Her hair is raven-wing black. She has large brown eyes that peer out from behind a cute oval face. She looks at me. I look at her. She smiles with embarrassment and looks away.

Grandmother is here, too. She wears a white peasant blouse with a gray shawl slung over one shoulder. Two gold coins made into earrings dangle from slightly stretched earlobes. She has steel-gray hair and deep weathered lines etch her bronzed face. She appears to have been the kind of woman who may have ridden with Poncho Villa, a woman fighting for the liberty of her country. And by the way her shawl is slung across her chest; it might just as well have been a brace of bandoliers.[1]

L. Factual vs. Emotional Truth, Observations From My Journal

This is an example of a writer; in this case me, observing in an objective matter a small family waiting in an airport lounge. At first it appears that I as a writer have taken no judgmental position. All I am doing is reporting in an objective, unemotional manner the facts I notice about a family. But am I truly without a bias?

They are a family of five, mother, father, two boys and a girl. The children are stair-step. Each, including mother and father are chewing great wads of gum. They seem like a hangdog family. All wear faded jeans. The boy wears a scuffed pair of

1 Hugh Steven, *Behind the Story* (Langley, B.C. Canada, Credo Publishers, 1986), p. 28,29.

Adidas with a dirty yellow tongue that hangs out through a lattice of soiled untied laces.

The mother's hair is piled up in a beehive style and looks as if at any moment it might collapse and release a torrent of angry bees. She wears a rumpled brown corduroy jacket and high-heeled sling-back pumps. They all wait in the airport lounge with faded luggage and an equally faded faraway look in their tired eyes.

This third observation comes from my vacation journal on our yearly trip to the Gulf Islands off the coast of British Columbia, Canada:

It's Sunday morning. I am sitting on a wooden deck looking out over the sea. The wind continually changes the face of the sea. At first there are sparkling diamonds gleaming in the warm morning sunlight. The deck commands a 360-degree view. If I turn to my left there is a great glade of forest pine trees that are shedding and dropping their pine cones that clunk and thud on the cottage roof and wooden deck. In front, the land slopes forward toward the sea all brown with wonderful dry, spindly, sun-scorched island grasses. A phalanx of great pines, fir and arbutus (madrona) trees stand like sentinels at the edge of the bank. Below the bank, the sea is ebbing. There are large flat rocks that form shallow tide pools. A heron stands stone still in the middle of one of the tide pools. He or she is blue-gray with a football-shaped body, a blue-crested head and long legs and a bill that without warning is suddenly thrust into the shallow pool in search of breakfast. Earlier this morning, four otters, and then a big sea lion, fished and frolicked in the channel waters. And coming in and out of my vision are white winged scoters, Brandt's cormorants, grebes and the ever-present glaucous gulls whose changing calls and body language are a never-ending source of delight.

It is an altogether exquisitely beautiful day. The sun is warm, but not overly hot. The sky is blue, bluer than robin's eggs. Last night the full moonlight cast a flood of light throughout the pine forest and a silvery path across the sea. I wonder if King David saw the same kind of moonlight when he wrote Psalm 102:25: "The heavens are the work of your hands."

1. Monday:

The magic of this place is that there is a different mood to each day. Morning and evening are seldom the same. The clouds and the sea and the weather are continually changing. This is a hauntingly beautiful place, like the melodies of a great symphony, like the music of many waters, like the sound and smell of first love. Today the sky is leaden, and the pewter sea is sloppy with occasional white caps that spray over the rocks. The rain has pelted the cabin roof and streaked the windows. The black iron stove with its one-eyed glass panel is glowing with the warmth of a mellow wood fire. It feels good to wear a sweater and drink a cup of steaming hot chocolate. As I look across the sea and the rugged rocky beach, it strikes me that this is almost unchanged since God first spoke and created this secluded corner of paradise.

2. Watching a Boat in a Stormy Sea

At first it was only a white dot on the horizon, like a child's toy boat bobbing high in the bathtub. But this was no bathtub. All night the wind has blown hard from the northwest. This is the direction of storms. The wind has churned the once-tranquil turquoise sea into an inky black slop. Wave after never-ending wave crashes onto the craggy sandstone shore with unabashed fury, and then recedes leaving gleaming white frothy foam as if drawing in its breath for yet another angry assault upon the shore.

And all the while the little boat comes closer and closer, plowing and straining against the heavy sea. First dipping out of sight, then riding the crest, then plunging below the great waves, and still it comes churning up its own gleaming salt spray from its bow while the sea seemed to be trying to flick this tiny white interloper off its breast.

In his book, *The Pleasure of Diaries,* Ronald Blythe wrote:

There are many pleasures to be gained from reading a diary; meeting extraordinary people from the past and watching them grapple with problems. Another is learning the rhythms of the past and how others live their daily lives.

One summer evening in 1873 the Rev. Kilvert wrote a lovely description of that day's sundown:

The corn seemed to be praising God and whispering its evening prayer. Across the great level meads came the martial music of a fife and drum band, and laughing voices of unseen girls were wafted from farms and hay fields out of the wide dusk.[1]

Some diaries are provocative for their brevity and lead to amazing wonders and speculations, like this from Lord Dufferin written on June 21, 1855:

The North Atlantic—Spanish Waves— (great Atlantic rollers)—Our cabin in a gale—Seasickness. From a scientific point of view—Wilson—a passenger commits suicide—First sight of Iceland—Floki of the Ravens—The Norse Mayflower—Faxa Fiord—We land in Thule.[2]

M. Journaling—A Way To Break Writer's Block

1 Ronald Blythe, *The Pleasure of Diaries,* (Insight, February 5, 1990) pp. 62,63.
2 Lord Dufferin, *Letters From High Latitudes,* (New York, R. Worthington, 1878) p 14.

Lord Dufferin's short terse words, jottings, or sketches seem at first to be woefully inadequate to be the foundation for a full-blown story of adventure and intrigue on the high seas. Yet the reality is that these jottings are enough to trigger Dufferin's memory to recall the full details of the event years later. They are, in fact, the reservoir from which he can draw the essence of a larger story. Lois Daniel in her book, *How to Write Your Own Life Story*, said." You will discover that one's memory will spark another and multiply itself many times. And it is from this wealth of material from which to write your story." Every writer I know, including myself, struggles sooner or later from writer's block. That feeling of utter malaise, self-doubt and a mocking inner voice that says, "What new thing can you tell anyone?" That's when I return to my journal, or the journals of others. I know that each person's life story is a kind of scripture waiting to be read and interpreted. Thus, one's journal, when written honestly and reflectively can reveal what it means to be human. When I read Lord Dufferin's journal I wanted to know how he felt standing on the deck of that schooner in a hurricane force wind. And what was the significance of the simple word "cabin?" Dufferin's fuller account of that incident taken from his expanded journal and written in rather prosaic language, nevertheless answered my questions and stirred my imagination:

> After being on deck for several hours in the presence of that tempest, -peering through the darkness at those black liquid walls of water, mounting above you in ceaseless agitation, or tumbling over in cataracts of gleaming foam—the wind roaring through the rigging, timbers creaking as if the ship would break its heart—the spray and rain beating in your face—everything around in tumult—suddenly to descend into the quiet of a snug, well-lighted cabin, with the firelight dancing on the white rose-bud chintz, the well-furnished bookshelves, and all the innumerable knick-knacks that decorate its walls, everything about you as bright and fresh as a lady's boudoir in May Fair, and the certainty of being a good three hundred miles from any troublesome shore, all combine to inspire a feeling of comfort and security difficult to describe.

While Lord Dufferins fuller description of his perilous voyage taken from his journal ignites our adventurous spirit and gives us a unique feel for a storm at sea, the real value is for Dufferin himself. His journal notes marked a fixed and unique moment in time he never wanted to forget and this is the nature of journaling story telling.

Chapter Ten
Words are More Than Sounds

The Sovereign Lord has given me an instructed tongue to know the word that sustains the weary, (Isaiah 50:4 NIV).

A Word Choice and Meaning

In an attempt to understand the nature of human speech, Lewis Carroll in his book *Alice in Wonderland*, has Humpty Dumpty say, with a rather scornful tone:

> When I use a word it means just what I mean it to say, nothing more or less.

However, if Humpty Dumpty is writing for a popular audience he has to be certain he uses words that communicate the same meaning to the receiver (reader) as he, the writer or speaker intended. Language is not always exact and precise. It is, in fact, infinitely malleable. Words are symbols of real things and are open to a variety of interpretations and cultural assumptions. The language of love for example has always been a series of coded signals that are often difficult to read. What is the encoded message behind the action of a man giving a dozen red roses to his girlfriend?   In themselves the roses are of little importance except as a symbol of transcendence. The young man gives roses to symbolize his romantic interest. To an older person the roses remind the man's wife or significant other of a special moment in the past that transcends the roses.   Therefore, understanding the denotative (core or dictionary) meaning and the connotative (emotional) meaning of the words (and actions, verbal and nonverbal) is a vital part of writing with clarity and meaning. It's helpful to remember the meaning of a word lies embedded in the cultural habits of a specific group and within an individual's nervous system and the association of words with one's life experiences.

If I say the word *bread* the image of, color, size, shape, weight, texture, taste and smell is not universal for everyone. People from different cultural and geographical backgrounds will have different images and feelings about the letters that make up that word. If a dentist says, "root canal," or if a doctor uses the language of his training and says words like, "sickness, hospital, surgery," those words can arouse such an emotional response that a person hears them as a death sentence. The dentist and the doctor on the other hand, associate these words with healing, health and life. Thus, if Humpty Dumpty uses a word that is clear in his own mind without regard to the emotional association that may cluster around that word, his message, will, like himself, be scrambled.

During the Iran hostage negotiations, the then U.S. Secretary of State, Cyrus Vance, intending to signal the belief that U.S.-Iran problems could be resolved, spoke of restoring *normal* diplomatic relations. Iran mistakenly took that to mean a return to things as they were under the despised Shah. After the U.S. realized its mistake, one State Department official said, "Sending diplomatic signals is like sending smoke signals in a high wind."

1. Check Beneath the Surface of Words

For these reasons I often make certain I understand the core or dictionary meaning of words I have chosen as well as their connotative (emotional) meaning. For example, I have no emotional attachment to the British swear word *bloody*. This is a word once used as a polite oath by 18th century upper class Englishmen. In the 19th century, the word was adopted by the lower class and the term became a forceful, impolite expression associated with violence and uncouth behavior. Thus, it's important to get into the habit of checking beneath the surface, or behind the face of a word to make certain the word conveys the precise meaning intended by the writer.

For this reason, I believe a writer should take all the time necessary to carefully craft his or her prose. The late Norman Cousins, who cared much about good writing said:

> Clean precise writing or speaking requires systematic sequential thought. Words have to be crafted not sprayed. They need to be fitted together with infinite care.

B. Going Beyond Technique and Rules

The act of communication should open a clear window of understanding from the heart and mind of the writer to that of the reader. However, to create that special connection between writer and reader it is wise to consider the words of Canadian artist Emily Carr who said:

> Be careful that you do not write or paint anything that is not your own, that you don't know in your own soul.

When you dig your own cisterns, and write from out of your own deep feelings, experiences and convictions, your words will come alive and pulsate with that extra artistic dimension that goes beyond mere technique and rules.

South African writer and world traveler Laurens Van der Post reminds us that, "A movement toward new meaning demands that *truth be lived before it can be known.*" I believe when a writer strives to interpret new truths from first-hand common experiences of life and turn them on their head, then the writer moves out of the realm of rules and technique into art.

This of course, gets us back to Humpty Dumpty who tells us that when he uses a word, it means exactly what he meant it to say. This can be either inspiring or hurtful, particularly if he meant to compliment a woman and used the wrong word from the little ditty that says:

> You can call a girl slender, but not skinny, you may call her a kit-
> ten but not a cat, a mouse but not a rat, a duck, but not a goose,
> a vision but not a sight.

David W. Augsburger, writing in Fuller Seminary's *Theology News and Notes*, answers the Humpty Dumpty question best when he says:

> I encode my experience in my expressions of my perceptions to
> translate my vision of life into a common language that may
> connect with yours. My meanings may meet your meanings
> across the bridge of words and, for moment, we commune. If
> either of us fails, you will not hear the meaning in me, though
> you catch every word. And I will mistake the meaning in you
> though I can repeat you word for word.[1]

C. Being Clear (comprehensible), Concise and Coherent

I love language, I love words, and I love books that contain words made into sentences that are clear, concise and coherent. And I love sentences that contain descriptive images that clearly and without ambiguity help me see what the author saw and felt. Note the sentence from Steven Callahan's book *Adrift*:

> Heavy tattooed arms pulled aboard hawsers thick as thighs and
> whipped them around the capstans.[2]

A younger reader might have difficulty with the words, hawser and capstans, but the average reader knows exactly what is happening. There is no need to puzzle, decode, reread and wonder who the actors are. The writer is like a painter daubing paint on a canvas to create a scene. So too, the writer paints scenes and images through the nuances of language, and the power of words correctly chosen. An executive with a New York advertising agency said:

Words, when spoken well or artfully written causes your cus-
tomer [reader] to see things in his or her mind [or imagination]
that you want him or her to actually experience. This is why

1   David W. Augsburger, *On Becoming a Writer*, (Pasadena, Fuller Theological Seminary, Theology News and Notes, December 1999), p. 8.
2   Steven Callahan, *Adrift Seventy-Six Days Lost At Sea* (New York, Ballantine Books, 1986), p. 95.

your choice of words is singularly vital to the success of your ads [your prose].

Some in academic circles hold to the notion that since nothing in life is simple, to write clearly is somehow being shallow. To use turgid or obscure language and syntax is supposed to signal a superior intellect and thus equal profundity. My response is simply that incomprehensibility is never a sign of a great writer.

D. Words Are More than Sounds

Most people understand that words are more than sounds. As children, we were terribly wrong when we used to chant, "Stick and stones may break my bones, but names will never hurt me." Words can bruise, hurt and sting. King David knew this when he wrote in Psalm 64:3:

They cut me down with sharpened tongues; they aim their bitter words like arrows straight at my heart.

Anyone who has been victimized by abusive or careless language knows that hurt feelings or a broken heart can take longer to heal than a broken bone. Many television comedy shows use abusive humor to generate laughter at another's expense. Referring to himself as a "clown," Dick Van Dyke, said, "I am strongly opposed to the modern trend of cruelty in humor. I think comedy should be gentle, human and tender."

1. The Put-Down

I was once the breakfast guest of a colleague, a Ph.D. professor at a prestigious university. My friend had the respect and admiration of his academic community and in every way seemed in control and at peace with himself. As we concluded breakfast a younger colleague joined our table. Almost immediately my friend and the younger man began a game of bantering—all in the name of good fun. Then the younger man made a joking reference to a supposed chink in the professor's intellect. Immediately I saw my friend's jaw tighten, his face became red and the bantering came to an abrupt end. His academic credentials notwithstanding, my friend was clearly bruised. At best, we humans are fragile, full of self-doubt, and need to be affirmed no matter how important or accomplished we appear to others. For this reason I believe "put-downs" are against God's intention for interpersonal relationships. Proverbs 12:18 reminds us that, "Reckless words pierce like a sword, but the tongue of the wise brings healing." Paul echoes this by saying:

Do not let any unwholesome talk come out of your mouth, but only what is helpful for the building up of others according to their needs (Ephesians 4:29).

Words are indeed more than mere sounds. To the Jewish mind the spoken word was alive and energized with power. Psalm 33 tells us that, "By the word of the Lord the heavens were made and all the hosts by the breath of his mouth." And by the word of the Lord, Lazarus was restored back to life.

2. Words Doing What They Say

We know that spoken words often do what they say. Words can humiliate, and be instruments of confusion and disorder. If a parent repeatedly tells a child he is stupid, ugly, lazy or slow, that child will indeed become what they are told. By contrast, one of the most powerful tools a parent can have for continuing creativity in a child's life is to affirm and praise him or her face-to-face. And a more powerful way yet, is to praise the child to a friend when the child thinks the parent doesn't know he or she is listening. The secret is to praise the child for a specific thing.

3. The Power of Words to Heal

One of the most interesting case studies of the power of words to heal was recorded by Dr. Bernard Lown, Professor of Cardiology, Harvard University of Public Health. One morning Dr. Lown, with a group of interns visited a critically ill man who had had a massive heart attack. The patient's cardiac muscle function was irreparably compromised.

Additionally, the man had an uncontrollably rapid heart rate and rhythm along with congested lungs. The patient was wearing an oxygen mask when Dr. Lown entered the patient's room. After examining the man Dr. Lown turned to the interns and said, "Mr. U had a wholesome, very loud third-sound gallop." The interns all nodded. Actually, a third-sound gallop is a poor sign and denotes the heart muscle is straining and usually failing.

However, the patient was seemingly unmindful of the dialogue across his bed and in a few days he slowly and unexpectedly began to improve and eventually was discharged from the hospital. Some weeks later Dr. Lown saw this man in his office for a checkup and said:

> I marveled at this man's recovery and asked about the basis for the miraculous improvement. 'Doctor,' said the man, 'I not only know what got me better, I even know the exact moment when it happened. I was sure I was near the end and you and your staff had given up hope. However, on Thursday morning when you entered with your troops something happened that changed everything. You listened to my heart, you seemed pleased by the findings and announced to all those standing around my bed that I had a 'wholesome gallop.' I knew the doctors, in talking to me might try to soften the thing up. But I knew they wouldn't kid each other. So when I overheard you tell your colleagues that I had a "wholesome gallop," I figured I still had a lot of kick to my heart and could not be dying. For the first time my spirits were lifted and I knew I would live and recover.[1]

I realize some physicians might treat this as an interesting anecdote without giving it too much credibility, just as some in the medical establishment might downplay the effective way Patch Adams used humor as a therapeutic tool. The wise man in Proverbs said, "Pleasant words are a honeycomb, sweet to the soul and healing to the bones."

E. Writing With Simplicity Without Sacrificing Complexity

A central theme throughout this book has been a call to prune one's prose of unnecessary words, verbosity and sacred clichés. In a variety of different ways I have said the most effective way to clearly and accurately communicate the meaning of your message is to use simple declarative sentences using Anglo-Saxon words that burst with flavor and that create a direct pictorial image in the reader's mind. Single words like roar, shriek or boom make your prose more emotionally satisfying

---

1   Bernard Lown, M.D. The Lost Art of Healing, (New York, Ballantine Books, 1999), p. 13ff.

to the reader than the phrase, "an incredibly loud noise." Beginning writers often feel they need to use high-sounding adjectives or long variants or pile adjectives one upon another to impress an audience with their cleverness. The reality is writing with simplicity and subtlety without sacrificing complexity is difficult but in the end produces the most powerful writing. Notice the flowing paragraph by H.E. Bates:

> An old man with steel-rimmed spectacles and very dusty clothes sat by the side of the road. There was a pontoon bridge across the river and cars, and trucks, and men and women and children were crossing it. The mule-drawn carts staggered up the steep bank from the bridge with soldiers helping push against the spokes of the wheels. The trucks ground up and away heading out of it all and the peasant plodded along in the ankle deep dust. But the old man was too tired to go any farther.[1]

This tiny war portrait is free from overblown rhetoric and war jargon. There are no vacant phrases that have only a broad meaning and depend on further explanation to paint the scene and add color and vitality to the prose. The paragraph is complete in itself.

F. Clichés

By definition, a cliché is a word or phrase that has been overused, or overexposed to the point of banality. The trouble with words like, *spine chilling, eerie, and black as coal,* said one writer "is that they are old and smooth and pass through the ear and the mind like warm wind." One person wrote (rather harshly) that the use of a cliché is the use of a ready-made, prefabricated formula designed to give those who are too lazy to think, the illusion of thinking. To reinforce this point, the person offered the following exchange from a Doonesbury cartoon in which a United States senator was supposedly being interviewed.

> Question: Senator, will your committee be learning any new evidence this week about the—affair?

---

1 H. E. Bates, *The Modern Short Story,* (Boston, The Writer Inc, 1968), p. 168.

Answer: Of course not. This is not a public hanging, nor is it a whitewash. I hate to take the wind out of your sails. But our sole purpose is to separate the smoke from the fire.

We don't want to scale a mountain of evidence only to find that it doesn't amount to a hill of beans. We've been down that road before and it's a minefield.

Question: Senator, will the committee be looking for any new metaphors?

Answer: No. I won't have these hearings turned into a witch-hunt for silver linings.

1. Jargon and Buzzwords

Jargon or buzzwords are often used as coded signals identifying that an individual is on the "inside" of a particular social or professional group. And of course, people in a specialized field make up new words and terms to deal with concepts that are exclusive to their particular disciplines. The most notable of these are people in the computer industry, the sports world and the military. And not to be outdone are teenagers who use buzzwords to identify themselves as belonging to a social peer group and to define their cliques. Another use for teenage jargon is the need to exclude others not in their group, including parents.

Consider the word "interface." It was once a noun but is now a verb meaning personal interaction. When you once asked a person how they felt they might have used a sports term and said, *I not feeling up to par.* Now such a person *is not on-line.* Some popular expressions in the nineties were *relevant, viable* and *innovative.* And a word used by many sophisticated business people in the late nineties was, *unpack it for me,* meaning to explain the concept more fully.

The difficulty with using trite expressions or buzzwords is that language changes and words like, *bummer, nerd, neat, where the rubber meets the road, laid back, off the wall,* and *humongous* can date your prose just as disastrously as if you used words like, *let's get down to brass tacks, poppycock and fiddlesticks* (meaning to express disgust).

2. Spiritual Language

I am aware that many twenty-first century church-going young people, or so called Generation Y, have often OD'd on the *spiritual* language of the Christian sub-culture. Many religious leaders, teachers and preachers are guilty of using religious jargon that carries zero meaning to young people born in the 1980s. In a tongue-in-cheek article by Dennis W. Roberts entitled *Bring on the Bromide Seltzer* he cites such phrases as *share* (Christians do not tell, they *share*). And *losing the victory*. From his *Pulpit Platitudes* section we get such phrases as, *deep truths* (up till now I've just been dishing up shallow truths) and *burdened with the cares of this world*. His section on *Promotional Puffery*, "Evangelistic Epithets" includes such phrases as, *Catch the Vision, I trust that—, Let's Believe Together for—, Come Expecting a Miracle and Love Offering* (as opposed to a hate offering).[1]

There are, of course, many other communities besides Christians that are guilty of using outdated language. One of the most notorious of these is the movie industry. Note the dialogue of a grade B swashbuckler movie:

Say the word your highness, and I'll pluck the feathers from this "Golden Hawk." Or, I speak no more, Varnoff! My sword speaks for me! En Garde!

G. Figures of Speech

The challenge that religious commentators face is how to talk about personal faith, trust in God, sin, salvation, judgment, the Kingdom and more, in an attractive and compelling way. How, in fact, to go beyond cerebral theological language, outdated catches phrases and cliches that have lost their force and emotional edge. The use of story and narrative is one of the best ways to teach a lesson or transmit an idea or feeling. Another way to give written prose an emotional edge and create mental pictures of light and shadow is by making creative use of common figures of speech.

1. Metaphor

In simple terms, metaphor is a figure of speech in which one object is assumed to be so like another that the characteristic of the one is attrib-

---

1   Dennis W. Roberts, *Bring on the Bromide Seltzer!* (*Eternity*, April 1980), p. 22,ff.

uted to the other. *Bob is a rat* is a metaphor. The power of metaphor is that it allows the writer to clothe abstract ideas into comprehensible, vibrant and colorful language.

2. Simile

Next to metaphor, *simile* is one of the two most frequently used figures of speech. A simile expresses a comparison between two things of different kinds or quality. Simile is always introduced by "like" or "as." *Bob is like a rat* is a simile. One caution is that similes should not be drawn between things that have too near and obvious resemblance to the object compared. One of the pressures in the act of comparing lies in discovering likeness where at first glance there appears to be none. Discovery makes the reader feel as though he or she has learned a delightful lesson. *She's as short and dark as a mid-winter day.*[1]

3. Irony

The ability to recognize irony requires a certain intelligence and sophistication. Not every writer can handle irony well. But for those who have a special capacity and interest, irony can be a powerful tool. Irony is simply the deliberate use of words or phrases to create an effect opposite to their literal meaning. Perhaps the most famous ironic imprint is Mark Antony's speech over the dead body of Caesar:"

> Come I to speak in Caesar's funeral. He was my friend, faithful and just to me: *But Brutus says he was ambitious; and Brutus is an honorable man.*

4. Hyperbole

When an English gentleman comes inside soaking wet after being in a torrential downpour and says, "It's a wee bit damp out there," he is using hyperbole to understate the facts. One of the most celebrated uses

---

1   There are many more useful examples of figures of speech than I have given in this section. For those interested in a fuller treatment of this subject I recommend the fourth edition of A *Handbook to Literature* by C. Hugh Holman, published by Bobbs-Merrill Educational Publishing Company, Indianapolis, 1980. I also recommend the excellent article *Watch Your Figure* by John Stewart, published in the April 1970 issue of *The Writer* from which I have drawn some of these illustrations.

of understatement came from Henry Stanley when, while extending his hand said, *Dr. Livingston, I presume.*

When a writer uses hyperbole, the reader should be sophisticated enough to know that exaggeration or understatement is not to be taken literally. The understood purpose of the figure of speech is to grab the reader's attention by the use of a vivid exaggeration. Some examples (clichés all) are, *I'm so hungry I could eat a horse. I have enough work for a month of Sundays. It's raining cats and dogs.* And a classic bit of hyperbolic rhetoric came from Norman Mailer describing the power of Muhammad Ali's punch. *His huge left hook was enough of a club to split a tree.*

While hyperbole is an interesting literary device, and an artful way of getting at the essential truth of things, I suggest caution. It is, after all an instrument of untruth. And some readers may not recognize the literary distinction of exaggeration for emphasis. This is one reason why it's important for writers to know their audience.

5. Antithesis

One of my favorite figures of speech is paradoxical antithesis. Unlike metaphor or simile, the meaning is found not in resemblance but in contrast. Jesus and the gospel writers made liberal use of antitheses by placing two unlike things side by side to create an emotional thump in the reader's mind and heart. For example:

If anyone would be first, be must be last (Mark 9:35).

Whoever would save his life must lose it (Mark 8:35).

Whoever would be the greatest among you must be your servant (Mark 10:43).

The practical rule of antithesis is to give the contrasted ideas a similar verbal construction. Contrast nouns with nouns, adjectives with adjectives and verbs with verbs. The agreement of the words in the contrasted clauses must be as nearly alike as possible.

H. Negatives

If getting rid of jargon means ejecting pretentious words and phrases for simple ideas, then the same rule applies to getting rid of negative language. The task of the writer is to make prose interesting and enjoyable. This means freeing the reader from having to reread a passage to decode its meaning.

Psychologist Hubert H. Clark, from Johns Hopkins University writing in the September 1974 issue *of Psychology Today* discovered that it takes the average person about 48% longer to understand a sentence using a negative, than it does to understand a positive or affirmative sentence. After I read that statement, I read 1 Timothy 5:9 in the New American Standard Bible that said:

Let a widow be put on the list if she is not less than sixty years old—having been the wife of one man.

At first reading I had trouble understanding the author's intention and meaning. I wasn't sure at what age a woman should be put on the widow's list and so had to read the verse again. Then I read the same verse from the J.B. Phillips translation:

Widows for your church list should be at least sixty years of age, should have had only one husband, and have a well-founded reputation for having lived a good life.

Note the difficulty of clearly understanding Romans 8:9 from William Barclay's translation:

> But you are not ruled by your lower nature, you are ruled by the Spirit, if it is true that the Spirit of God has really made a home in you. *No one who does not possess the Spirit belongs to Christ.*

Notice the problems of negatives in this British pamphlet on pensions and insurance:

> A Class I contribution is not payable for employment by any employer for not more than eight hours in any week—but if you normally work for more than eight hours in any week for any one employer, a Class I contribution is payable except for any week you do not do more than four hours of work for that employer.

We have difficulty understanding this mental tangle because we have to decode at least four negatives, three nots and one except. When we hear or read the sentence, "John isn't home," we treat it mentally as, Not plus John is home. Breaking the sentence into two entities instead of one takes more time. In the "True or False" test where the phrase, "Nine is not an even number," Clark demonstrated the negative took people more than a half-second longer to verify than it did an affirmative sentence. This may seem to be a trivial amount of time to quibble over, but if you are answering a quiz question on Jeopardy, it could mean the difference between success or failure to win a million dollars.

Morley Safer of the famed *Sixty Minutes* once accused former Secretary of State Alexander Haig as a man who changes verbs into nouns. Safer then quoted Haig as saying: *This is not an experience I haven't been through before.* In a Los Angeles airport restaurant I noticed a sign that said, *it is not impolite to pass if there is a vacant space in line.*

In the article in *Psychology Today*, Clark said, "A person should not never use a negative (no, not never)." Clark stressed that most people find it easier to think in positive terms than in negative ones.

1. Hidden Negatives

Curiously some words in the English language only hint at their negativism by the prefix "un" as in uncork, or "dis," as in disengage. But other words like absent, different, hardly, scarcely, few, leave, doubt, error, and wasted time hide and never tell you they are from the negative family. Interestingly, Clark demonstrated that the word absent takes longer to comprehend than the word present.

I. Euphemisms

What do the phrases, (1) "He has undergone the ultimate maturation" (2) "Protective reaction strike?" (3) "Content-provider and (4) "Negative saver," have in common? Yes, you are correct, they are euphemisms. Number 1 is a euphemism for death. Most people, including doctors, clergymen, or undertakers (known as morticians), will not admit a person has died. Rather, *they have expired, passed away, or they are no longer with us.*

Number 2 was a euphemism for bombing. This was a term used in the Vietnam war to soften public opinion for the air strikes in Cambodia. During the Gulf war the U.S. military softened the horror of foreign civilians being killed by U.S. bombs with the use of the chilling euphemism, *collateral damage* when they were striking tactical targets, (read, the enemy or the attackers). Number 3 is, (in my opinion) a put-down for writer. And number 4 is a phrase invented by a Washington economist to describe people who spend more money than they make.

To be sure, euphemisms have their place, since they substitute a pleasant word for a more blunt one. Americans have no difficulty using the word, restroom, comfort station, lavatory, or in Latin America, water closet, or just WC for the blunt word "toilet." The British like to play little jokes on their American guests and indeed escort them to the bathroom, when the guest might need a toilet since in most British homes these are in separate rooms.

Creating euphemisms dates back to the Norman Conquest in 1066. At that time the community began to make a distinction between genteel and obscene vocabulary, between the Latin words of the upper class and the lusty Anglo-Saxon words of the lower class. That is why a duchess perspired, expectorated and menstruates, while a kitchen maid, sweated, spat and bled.

Euphemisms are interesting figures of speech, and if you wish to call a janitor a custodian, or a garbage man a sanitary engineer, no harm is done. In fact you may have boosted their self-esteem. But if you write about substandard housing when in fact they are rotting slums, then you have distorted the ability of your readers to assess the true significance of poverty in a particular community.

I do understand the need for diplomacy in certain circles. If you are the guest of a certain government, it is generally unwise to write newsletters to one's constituents about the squalid slum conditions of a particular city. There are, however creative ways to talk about such issues without a frontal attack on one's host country. Wycliffe founder Cameron Townsend faced such an issue early in his ministry. Rather than throw verbal jabs at the government, Townsend creatively wrote a novel that examined the everlasting conflict that exists between historical and social events, and the plight of ethnic minorities who are caught in the middle or on the cusp of society.

1. Being an Instrument of Your Time

At issue however, is the responsibility of a writer, writing within his or her own culture to be true to the nature of language and the reality of things as they are. Paul Johnson author of *Modern Times, Intellectuals and Birth of the Modern* said, "One of the sources of evil in the modern world has been the devaluation of language." By this he meant that in the hands of totalitarianism, language becomes the instrument of falsification instead of enlightenment and hope. "In my opinion," said one writer, "Any writer who falsifies reality destroys himself, (herself) as a writer." The major theme and concern in the writings of Alexander Solzhenitsyn is with the soul of man and the effect evil and good, truth and falsehood have on the human soul. He believes it is the duty and purpose of an artist to serve his readers by writing truth. He once wrote:

> Without moral purpose there is no artist, and there is no literature.

The challenge I give to myself and to all who have a personal "I-thou" commitment to the God of creation is to be his instrument within our own time and frame of reference. Remember C.S. Lewis's statement. *The moral inherent in your books will rise from whatever spiritual roots you have succeeded in striking in the course of your* life.

Chapter Eleven

A Potpourri of Tips to Ponder

A. You Are What You Do

Little is accomplished without enthusiasm and a fundamental self-confidence in one's ability to complete a writing project. It's important therefore to remind yourself if you write, you are indeed a writer. If you are one who works with words, then don't be afraid to call yourself by the name that distinguishes what it is you do. Then tell yourself you have the confidence, talent and determined discipline to create the work that you know is in you. P.D. James once said:

You must write, not just think you're going to. And you must widen your vocabulary and enjoy words. You must read widely not in order to copy, but to find your own voice. It's a matter of going through life with one's senses alive, to be responsive to experiences, and to other people.

B. Creativity

One of the first things to say about the nature of creativity is that it's not found in a formula. Rather, creativity is highly individualistic and involves a way of thinking, looking and listening unique to the individual. While many agree that creativity is something of a mystery, educators, artists and professionals believe people can be creative if they wish. After all, to be human is to be creative. However, creativity often needs to be awakened. This occurs when we give ourselves permission to open doors that have been locked or closed off.

Creativity involves the uncensored flow of thoughts, images and imagination. Creativity also involves a synthesis of knowledge, intuition and skill that transforms the creative impulse into the creative act. Think about the sailor who was afraid of falling off the edge of the world into nothingness, or of encountering sea monsters if he went beyond the horizon. Following the creative path is often difficult and frightening.

Creativity then is a process of synthesizing existing facts, ideas, and intuitive feelings, that when incubated, tumble over in one's head, and when stood on end produces what Ray Bradbury said was a "continual surprise." To be sure, creativity is difficult to explain and may appear to others to be entirely irrational but it is the essential component for creative expression.

C. Biography

The simplest definition of biography is that it is the history of an individual's life written by another person. The task of the biographer is to explore the various regions of a character's life and out of the building blocks of the character's experiences, feelings and reflections create a coherent narrative with a beginning, middle and ending. It is helpful to remember that English biography had its roots in hagiography. The purpose of hagiography was to praise the exploits of some noble personage without mentioning their faults or weaknesses. How times have changed! Most modern biographies relate "warts" and all. People are human and readers should be able to relate to the character as a human being.

Thus faults and mistakes in judgment should be shown and discussed as well as accomplishments. My own *modus operandi* is that to the extent a person's domestic life impinges on their public life and accomplishments, I try to deal with their faults, weaknesses and misjudgments sympathetically but not defensively. If there are family members of the principal character still living, the biographer ought to deal with private matters delicately and with common sense. In a word, I want my biography to be both truthful and edifying.

D. Elements of Story

A story is an account of characters and events in a plot moving over time and space through conflict toward resolution. All stories involve some kind of search, struggle or problem, a battle of contending forces or ideas that has to be resolved. And, of course, if story involves a search or quest, there has to be a searcher (character(s).

I believe a good story follows aesthetic laws that are part of God's created order. We see this most clearly in Fairy Tales where eternal values like *truth, honesty, fair play, beauty, courage, perseverance* and *good versus evil* are interwoven to produce a satisfying conclusion. A good story is one where the reader participates imaginatively in the unfolding action. It's helpful to remember that both Christian and non-Christian writers are bound to the same standards of literary craftsmanship. The amazing things about the stories by J.R.R. Tolkien's *Lord of the Rings* and C.S. Lewis's *Chronicles of Narnia* is that they have been accepted by hundreds of thousands of readers who have rejected religion. And while there is no overt religion in these books, the books are all religion and they are good, gripping stories.

E. The Plot

Plot should be like a picture and have structure. Characters in a plot do not deal in generalities. They must want something or do something in particular. If you merely have a series of conflicts that are unrelated to a story line then all you have are isolated episodes. The action of a story must lead to some kind of satisfactory conclusion.

F. Editing

Written material set in type only seems perfect. All writers know that when they place that final period of the last sentence there is always something that could have been expressed just a little better. In an article by Martin Marty on the question of copy-editing he said, "Copy-editing, is an art I revere, a craft I need and a science I have not mastered." I am very much in Martin Marty's camp.

At first blush, one's solution or series of words in an article may seem correct, but on reflection is discarded for something better. Editors and writers know that for a greater degree of self-evaluation it's important to stand back from one's work and return after a period of "cooling off" to re-write and tighten one's work. The careful writer knows every word, every anecdote, every quote; every statistic should in some way support, relate and advance the story. Anything that does not do this should be left out, no matter how attractive it is in itself.

G. Details

Steven Callahan in the preface to his book, *Adrift, Seventy-Six Days Lost At Sea* said, "As I prepared my outline for my book I divided notations from my log into two categories: *events,* and *ideas.* Under events I wrote down the details of the ships I saw, the fish I caught, the sharks I encountered. Under *ideas,* I wrote what I felt and thought about these events. From this I organized chapters that corresponded to the different stages of the voyage. Callahan then adds a bit of honest candor when he says, "I perceived at the time, of course, I could never be completely sure that all my conclusions are exactly what I felt rather than new insights."[1] The important point here is to make certain the details relate directly to the central point of your story.

H. Developing One's Spiritual (Writing) Life

There is similarity between developing one's spiritual life and one's writing life. As pragmatic as it sounds, you are the only one who can bring your story to life. In a word, you need to make it happen. Everything depends on your own mental attitude, which should include a passionate desire to think and to translate that thinking into prose with a certain amount of joy and aliveness. There is common agreement among seasoned writers that the more writers throw their imagination into their perceptions, the more alive they will feel toward their work. The death knell for any writer is to accept his or her world without desire and imagination. Writing, like one's spiritual life, is similar to a garden that needs to be nurtured, tended, watered, weeded and encouraged.

---

1   Steven Callhan, *Adrift, Seventy-Six Days Lost At Sea* (New York, Ballantine Books, 1986), p. XII.

I. Personal Writing Habits

Writing is an evolutionary process, a gradual transformation of random ideas and free-form thoughts and images that must be crafted into polished prose. Thus the composing process is ultimately a personal matter and each will adopt his or her own unique style or vision to the data.

Some writers like to write in longhand and later transfer their prose to the computer. While I use a computer, I sometimes write in longhand if I am stuck on a particular passage. Something happens creatively when I take a pen in hand and can feel the tactical weight of the pen on the hard surface of white bond paper. I suppose this is the reason Dawson Trotman, founder of the Navigators, was fond of saying, *Thoughts untangle and make more sense as they pass through articulating fingertips.*

Some writers write quickly without too much thought to spelling or grammar and even leaving certain passages incomplete as a way of getting the story out on paper. I have never been able to do this. I need to be satisfied that each paragraph or page is generally the way I want it before I can move on. I am, of course, open to editing and rewriting after I have completed the story. I am also aware that false starts and changes of direction in a story line are normal.

J. Outline

An outline is a road map that can be referred to as you write. It is not, however, like the law of the Medes and Persians that cannot, or never should be broken. One benefit for an outline, besides helping the writer get to where he or she wants to go, is that it may uncover areas in your story that need to be strengthened and flushed out.

Some writers work better from a detailed outline, others like to think long and hard before writing and then move quickly into a first draft with only a skeleton of an outline in their head. While I have a general idea where I want to go with a story, I sometimes have to write to find out where I am going. I am consciously aware that the weight of the story material has a life of its own and may lead and pull me in directions I never thought of or dreamed about when I first outlined my story. Once again, there is no right or wrong way to craft a story—just that you complete your project.

K. Interviewing and Listening

The most successful interviewers are those who have developed the discipline of listening. The person who listens sensitively can then ask the thoughtful, sensitive question that will bring ideas and feelings to mind. For the person who says they can't remember, use brief words and phrases to capture free-floating ideas. "Did you ever have a dog as a child?" "What was its name?" "What do you remember about your first day of school?" Edmund Morris who wrote *Dutch* the controversial biography of Ronald Reagan, used this method when he said:

> When I asked Ronald Reagan a question about himself it was like dropping a stone into a well and never hearing a splash.

Morris wasn't getting anywhere with his interviews until he showed Reagan a leaf and something clicked and Reagan began talking about his boyhood days.

A successful interview occurs when the interviewer is prepared well in advance of the interview with thoughtful intelligent questions. The other side of the coin is that an interviewer is not so tied to an outline or set of questions that he or she misses the serendipitous experience. The writer must always be *open for discovery.*

L. Clichés

By definition clichés are trite, hackneyed words or phrases that have lost their original force and emotional edge. Avoid them like the plague!

M. Observation

A writer can only discover the real thing through deliberate and purposeful accumulation of details. Thus, what matters most is how deeply you see, how attentively you hear, how richly the encounters are felt in your heart and soul. I wish all writers would be as observant and sensitive to their environment as was Steven Callahan. When he was rescued from his seventy-six days at sea by some fishermen off the Island of Guadeloupe he wrote:

The perfume of flowers and grasses blows off the island and wafts into my nostrils. I feel as if I am seeing color, hearing sounds, and smelling land for the first time. I am emerging from the womb again.[1]

N. Metaphor

Aristotle said, "Strange words simply puzzle us; ordinary words convey only what we already know. It is from metaphor that we can get hold of something fresh."

O. Imagination

When Albert Einstein said that imagination was more important than intelligence, he didn't mean imagination was a mental activity that one uses to "make things up." Einstein meant there could be no meaningful use of intelligence unless there is an imaginative perception or discriminating understanding between observation and thought. In other words, don't take everything you see at face value. All things are not as they seem. Instead use your imagination because this is the instrument of thought that turns observed experience into understanding.

William Blake, one of the great creative poets and thinkers of the nineteenth century, used the term *imagination* to denote man as an acting perceiving being. Like Einstein, Blake challenged men and women to use their imagination to see beyond facts, beyond the observable. He said:

Scientists should be trained to see the sun as fact: artists should see it emotionally as beautiful. [2]

Art is based on sense experience, but said Blake, "It is an imaginative ordering of sense experience that gives form and shape to one's art. The composition of music is an imaginative ordering of the sense experience of sound."

For Blake, imagination functioned as inspiration, which he said sometimes had a purpose and will independent of the artist.

P. Simplicity in Writing

---

1 *Ibid*, p. 217.
2 Northrop Frye, *Fearful Symmetry, A Study of William Blake*, (Princeton University Press, 1990), p. 20, 24.

Those who know they are profound, strive for clarity. Those who would like to seem profound strive for obscurity.

Q. When To Start Your Writing Project

You begin writing (biography) when you feel you have a solid understanding of the ideas, purposes and motivation of your character. Also you must have internalized the facts and feel you know him or her as well as you know an intimate friend of many years.

R. What To Put in Your Story and What to Leave Out

The best advice I can give for what to put in and what to leave out of a biography or memoir comes from Natalie Rothstein who said, when she wrote her memoirs that she tried to be "authentic without being exploitive." After determining what it was that she wanted to say in her memoirs, Rothstein said:

I felt it was appropriate to omit the very personal if it were to cause pain, or if it seemed to me to be self-indulgent. There is always a dichotomy between honesty and discretion; too much of one, and the other suffers."[1]

S. Journaling

Most people journal to preserve their emotional memories or to get something off their chest. One also journals in the hope of expressing something beautiful, or to overcome frustration, or just for the sheer joy of taking an idea and exploring and developing it. A spiritual journal can help pinpoint those moments in time when God's grace, forgiveness, love, mercy and guidance become more compelling and real in one's life. The insights from one's journal can also be incorporated into one's prose, particularly during a time of dryness or writer's block.

T. Having a Room of One's Own

Writing is sometimes described as a muscle. The more you use it the more flexible and useful it becomes. I am also realistic enough to know that it is not practical, and perhaps not even useful to absolutely write every day. However, I believe it is important to have a regular or specific time and place in which to write. A dedicated work place, no matter how small, will create the right kind of mood and signal to the senses that it's now time to do serious work.

U. When Is the Best Time to Write?

Some writers prefer the morning, others late at night, or only when it rains. (I love writing on a cold rainy day with a cup of hot chocolate at the ready.) Some like a room that is perfectly quiet; others like to play classical music in the background. There are also people who write during the rush of life, writing on the backs of envelopes, some in the margins of their church bulletin when a thought suddenly struck them. Others like Ken Taylor, translator of the *Living Bible,* wrote while on a commuter train. Still others snatched a few moments in the afternoon while their baby took a nap.

Once again, there is no right or wrong way or time to write, only that you do whatever is necessary to complete the project. Remember too, that the so called muse, or inspiration comes out of being well prepared with a good set of notes and indexed research material.

V. Do You Need A Degree In Order to Write?

Two-time Pulitzer Prize winning historian and author Barbara Tuchman never earned a graduate degree. She wrote most of her eleven books while rearing three daughters.

W. Health

The media, Hollywood and others have often romanticized and glorified the hard-drinking macho image of several American Nobel Prize winners for literature like William Faulkner, Ernest Hemingway, John Steinbeck, Eugene O'Neill and Sinclair Lewis who wrote while abusing their bodies with drugs and alcohol. The reality is that such abuse caused the death and destruction of their talent. Writing is hard, intense, exhausting work. And in the words of Gabril Garcia Marquez, *to be a good writer you have to be absolutely lucid at every moment of writing, and in good health.* I am reminded that the qualities and discipline required to produce a true athlete are also the same for a true artist.

X. How to Face Rejection

It's not easy. Our egos, our self-esteem, self-worth and self-confidence become like exposed nerves. The best advice is to keep sending out your manuscripts and get back to work on another project. It is also helpful to remember the words from Rudyard Kipling's classic poem:

> If you can meet with Triumph and Disaster, and treat those two imposters just the same...You will be a man [woman] my son, [and a better and happier writer].

As in sport, the writer's greatest asset is a positive mental attitude, knowing what you want to accomplish, concentration, a good self-concept, persistence and lots of practice. But mixed in with the persistence and practice must also come times of relaxation. Excessive tension and anxiety can sabotage a writer's ability to think creatively and to do his or her best work. Allowing time for jogging, games, meditation, listening to music, seeing a good movie or play or entertaining dinner guests can be useful and productive ways to relieve tension and refresh the spirit.

Y. Remember Also:

1. Effective communication means cutting down the mental steps a reader has to go through in order to understand your message. The mind handles a positive statement easier than a negative.

2. Writers have an obligation to their readership to be clear, concise, coherent and accurate. Yet, while the wise writer strives for simplicity he or she does not sacrifice complexity.

3. Be specific in a concrete way. Use examples that give your reader a sense of place, of being there, of touching, smelling, seeing and *feeling* what you have experienced. After reading your article, essay, book, or whatever you have written, your reader should be able to see what you (the writer) had seen, what you felt and understood about the person, place or ministry you wrote about. The power and impact of your prose

comes ultimately from the imagery that grew out of your personal experiences, feelings and observations.

4. Creativity requires sensitivity, independence and works well when people work off the record. Agatha Christie said, "The best time for [thinking] planning a book is while you are doing the dishes." This supports the adage that ninety percent of the work of writing is internal, [and doing research] and only ten percent happens at the computer.

5. Force yourself to think more clearly by breaking long complex sentences into two, three, or more simple sentences. The average reader prefers a sentence length of 15-20 words.

6. The first point about the art of telling a story is that the story itself must grab your attention. Because if it doesn't it certainly won't grab your reader.

7. Writing is a craft, an art form learned by hard work.

8. Know your audience and decide before writing what kind of impact you want to make on your reader. Always have someone in mind as you write.

9. Use the active voice. Write with nouns and verbs.

"John hit Peter," is better than "Peter was hit by John."

10. Go on a "which" hunt, and omit needless words.

11. Never send in a first draft. Let your story cool, then return to revise and rewrite.

12. Avoid jargon and clichés. Write naturally; use short words from everyday speech. Don't be afraid to use figurative language that paints a picture.

13. Think as a scholar, as a wise person but communicate in the language of the people. Write with a clear and simple style that is mature in seriousness and tone and Christian perspective. The purpose is to help reawaken your audience to the vibrancy of faith and purpose.

14. Conspicuous by its absence is a word on how to actually get published. I suggest checking out *The Writer's Resource Handbook,* see (Bibliography). However, just as there is a single word to remember to help you complete the act of writing so too, must you remember the same word when it comes to submitting your manuscript for publication, that word is *perseverance,* or persistence.

15. Blocks to one's creativity can occur when one is subject to personal harassment, cynical criticism, and personal put-downs that block the free flow of one's true and deep inner feelings.

16. Unlike God's creativity, human creativity does not make something out of nothing. Human creativity works within the framework of what God has created. C. S. Lewis reminds us that. " An author should never conceive himself [herself] as bringing into existence beauty or wisdom which did not exist before, but simply and solely as trying to embody in terms of his or her own art some reflection of eternal Beauty and Wisdom. Yet innovation, spontaneity, and a pioneering free spirit mark great authors."

17. Stephen Oates said, "The pure biographer seeks to elicit from the coldness of fact, the warmth of a life being lived."

Nothing in the world can take the place of Persistence. *Talent will not; nothing is more common than unsuccessful men with talent. Genius will not; unrewarded genius is almost a proverb. Education will not; the world is full of educated derelicts. Persistence and determination alone are omnipotent.*[1]

---

1 C.S. Lewis, *Christian Reflections,* (Glasgow, Scotland, Collins, Fount Paperbacks, 1980), p. 22.

Bibliography And Further Reading

Bausch, William, J. *Storytelling, Imagination and Faith*, Mystic, Connecticut, Twenty-Third Publications, 1989.

Bradley, James E and Richard A. Muller, *Church History, an Introduction to Research, Reference Works and Methods*, Grand Rapids, Michigan, William B. Eerdmans Publishing Company, 1995.

Brown, Colin, *History and Faith*, Grand Rapids, Michigan, Zondervan Publishing House, 1987.

Carr, W.H. *What is History?* Great Britain, Penguin Books, 1961

Cousineau, Phil, *The Act of the Pilgrimage*, Berkeley, California, Conari Press, 1998.

Dillard, Annie, *The Writing Life*, New York, Harper & Row 1989.

Duriez, Colin, *A Field Guide To Narnia*, Downers Grove, Illinois, InterVarsity Press.

Elton, G.R., *The Practice of History*, London, 8 Grafton Street W1X 3LA Flamingo, Fontana Paperbacks, 1984

Evans, Richard J., *In Defense of History*, W.W. Norton & Company, New York, 1999.

Feller, Bruce, *Walking the Bible*, William Morrow, New York, 2001

Fountain, André and Galvin, William, A. Jr., *The Art of Writing Nonfiction*, New York, Syracuse, University Press, 1987.

Frye, Northrop, *The Educated Imagination*, Bloomington, Indiana University Press, 1964.

Frye, Northrop, *A Fearful Symmetry*, A Study of William Blake, Princeton University Press, 1990.

Gallager, Susan V. and Roger Lundin, *Literature Throught the Eyes of Faith*, San Francisco, Harper & Row, Publishers, 1989.

Gardner, John, *The Art of Fiction, Notes on Craft for Young Writers*, New York, Vintage Books, Random House, 1985

Goldberg, Natalie, *Writing Down The Bones*, Boston, Shambhala, 1986

Goodwin, Doris Kearns, *No Ordinary Time*, Franklin & Eleanor Roosevelt: The Home Front In World War II, New York, Touchstone, Simon & Schuster, 1995.

Grant Daniel, *The Writer's Resource Handbook*. New York, Allworth Press. 1996

Hayakawa, S.I. *Language In Thought And Action*, London, George Allen & Company LTD., 1996.

Hessler, Peter, *River Town: Two Years on the Yangtze*, New York, Harper Collins, 2001.

James, P.D. *Time To Be Earnest, a Fragment of Autobiography*, New York, Alfred A. Knopf, 1999.

William Kelleher, *Writing History, A Guide for Students, Second Edition*, New York, Oxford University Press, 2004.

Kenney, Dr. William, *How to Read and Write About Fiction*, New York, Simon & Schuster, Inc., 1996.

Lomask, Milton, *The Biographer's Craft*, New York, Perennial Library, Harper & Row, 1987.

Lopez, Barry, *About This Life: Journeys on the Threshold of Memory*, New York, Vintage Books, 1988.

Manchester, William, *A World Lit Only By Fire*, Boston, Little Brown & Company, 1992.

Mavrow, Cecila, *Journal Writing*, Victoria, Canada, Ruksak Books Ltd., 1992.

McNeil, Robert, *Woodstruck, A Memoir*, New York, Viking, 1989.

Noll, Mark A., *Turning Points, Decisive Moments In The History Of Christianity.* Grand Rapids. Michigan, Baker Books, 1987.

Ryken, Leland, *Triumphs Of The Imagination*, Downer's Grove, Illinois, Inter-Varsity Press, 1979.

Ryken, Leland, *How to Read the Bible as Literature, and Get More Out of It.* Grand Rapids, Michigan Zondervan Publishing House, 1984.

Shaw, Luci, *Life Path, Personal and Spiritual Growth Through Journal Writing*, Portland Oregon, Multnomah Press, 1991.

Spence, Linda, *Legacy, a Step-By-Step Guide to Writing Personal History*, Athens, Swallow Press/ Ohio University Press, 1997.

Taylor, Daniel, *The Healing Power of Stories*, New York, Doubleday, 1996.

Veith, Gene Edward Jr., Reading Between the Lines, A Christian Guide to Literature, Wheaton, Illinois, Crossway Books, A Division of Good News Publishers, 1990

Wells, Ronald, *History Through the Eyes of Faith*, San Francisco, Harper & Row, Publishers, 1989.

Wide as the Waters, The Story of the English Bible and the Revolution it Inspired, New York, Penguin Books, 2001.

Winchester, Simon, *The River At The Center Of The World, A Journey Up The Yangtze, And Back In Chinese Time*, New York, Picador, Henry Holt and Company, 2004.

Yancey, Phillip and James Calvin Schaap, *More than Words*, Grand Rapids, Michigan, Baker Books, 2002.

M

T